BEST
BEHAVIOUR

The Tatler Book of Alternative Etiquette

To my mother

BEST
BEHAVIOUR

The Tatler Book of Alternative Etiquette

MARY KILLEN

With illustrations by
ANNIE TEMPEST

CENTURY

London   Sydney   Auckland   Johannesburg

Design by Heather Johns

First published in 1990
by Century Editions an imprint of
The Random Century Group Ltd,
20 Vauxhall Bridge Road,
London SW1V 2SA

The Random Century Group Australia (Pty) Ltd,
20 Alfred Street, Milsons Point,
Sydney, NSW 2061, Australia

The Random Century Group
South Africa (Pty) Ltd,
PO Box 337, Bergvlei 2012,
South Africa

The Random Century Group New Zealand Ltd,
PO Box 40-086, 32-34 View Road,
Glenfield, Auckland 10, New Zealand

British Library Cataloguing in Publication data
Killen, Mary
Best behaviour: the Tatler book of alternative etiquette.
1. Great Britain. Etiquette
I. Title   II. The Tatler
395.0941

ISBN 0 7126 4545 4

Typeset by SX Composing Ltd, Rayleigh, Essex
Printed and bound in England by Clays, Norwich

CONTENTS

How can I prevent a bullying hooray from forcing everyone to play charades?

HOUSE PARTIES

HOSTING A HOUSE PARTY

IT IS MUCH GREATER to give than to receive. It is also, in the long term, more profitable. The goodwill bought by largesse will come back on a hostess tenfold. But largesse alone will not suffice when hosting a house party. It will be necessary to curtail your own irritability and anxiety levels as an atmosphere of tension and guilt must not be engendered amongst your guests.

Planning will pay satisfying dividends and a lightly structured timetable will be secretly acceptable to most guests. Though nine out of ten would assert verbally that they preferred to do their own thing, in reality humans enjoy structure (further reading: *The Fear of Freedom* by Erich Fromm). What's more, it is practical to accept the suggestions of a forward planner who is aware of the facilities available in the area.

As a hangover from teenagehood, however, timetables are linked in many minds with school and resentment may resurface if guests feel they are being 'bossed'.

Therefore your schedule should be disguised diurnally, as a set of impromptu suggested options. 'Some people are going over to Elgin Mills after lunch,' you might mention languidly to selected 'ringleaders'. 'Men won't be interested but they could go and stock up with wine while we're doing that and then we could all go on to see the Findhorn community, if anyone would like to.'

You will find the cars filling up nicely as the majority of guests comply with your 'suggestion'. Mental laziness takes a keener grip than ever when people are on holiday.

Those who don't fall into line should of course have no pressure exerted on them. This is particularly important with after-dinner games which many people find tiresome. If a hostess wishes to stage them, there should be a separate withdrawing room for those who do not wish to take part.

CHOOSING THE GUEST LIST
As a general rule it is more exciting to have a house party made up of slightly more men than women. Yet the paucity of

hetero sexual bachelors without personality disorders plagues even the most successful of hostesses.

This fact will be most cruelly apparent to hostesses with friends in the thirty- to forty-year-old age bracket, where the ratio is an average of twelve ravishingly beautiful, intelligent and rich single girls to every one possible suitor, usually a recently divorced man.

Normal men over thirty who have not been 'bagged' are at a premium and for this reasons houseparties pullulate with abnormal ones. Be they roués, sadists or alcoholics, be the evidence of their resolve to continue as bachelors clear as crystal, their popularity will nonetheless be paramount so long as they could, theoretically, serve as suitors to one of the single girls who may be present. Such men can pick and choose from the glut of invitations they will receive throughout the season.

The careful hostess will keep her eye on proceedings at the divorce courts or in turbulent relationships so that she may be ready to 'snap up' more promising single men coming on to the market for her float of potential invitees.

There are no other rules about configurations, but it is always amusing to invite at least one person who can play a musical instrument and at least one over-sexed guest.

PROMOTING INTIMACY BETWEEN SINGLE GUESTS

Q. Have you any tips for throwing people together without their suspecting? We have asked some people up next month and two of them would, I am sure, be wonderfully matched. Yet they are both rather diffident. How can I arrange it so that they spend some time alone together?   B.F., Kelso

A. *For these purposes hostesses should always keep a spare car, the insurance of which covers any driver. In this way it will be possible to stage expeditions through preferably isolated countryside, with the singles in question bringing up the rear. Arrange that their car has only enough petrol to take them to a certain key point, ideally four miles or so through beautiful countryside to the nearest place where they can get assistance. If they are attracted to one another they will seize the opportunity to walk to this point together when the car breaks down, and this should afford them the opportunity to develop their relationship in a suitable manner.*

THE FINANCING OF HOUSE PARTIES

Q. My husband and I have rather overstretched ourselves and have taken a fishing lodge attached to a ducal estate in Scotland for a week in August. We have invited twenty friends to stay but, following a recent stockmarket disaster, are really rather pushed for cash. Can you suggest any budgetary measures that might be taken? A.R.B., Crediton

A. *Many ducal estates who rent out fishing lodges do so because they too are strapped for cash. They therefore also open their houses to the public and provide refreshment facilities. For this purpose they are entitled to use a cash and carry card to obtain substantial discounts. The duke you refer to may well be happy to oblige by lending you his card so that you too might benefit from the savings available through bulk purchase.*

Another more despicable measure employed by one Gloucestershire house party host is to advise guests that tips should be left with him to be divided correctly. In this way he recoups some of the expenditure he has made and also ensures that his staff are not rendered dissatisfied by the wild variations in their income.

BULLYING HOORAYS TRYING TO MAKE OTHER PEOPLE PLAY CHARADES

Q. I am frightfully fond of a certain person whom I have invited to stay over Easter at our house in Yorkshire in a party of twenty. My only worry is that he may become overhearty after dinner and start bullying people to take part in charades. B.M., S.W.11

A. *The key moment is the interval between dinner ending and the withdrawing process, so why not assign him some duty such as shutting up chickens, checking on fires, closing gates or sawing frozen salmon for the following day so as to render him impotent until his potential victims have settled irrevocably into doing whatever other thing they might feel like?*

AN AMUSING NEW GAME FOR AFTER DINNER

Q. Are there any good new after-dinner games to enliven house parties? I am having fourteen people to shoot in Scotland at the end of the month. J.D., W.8

A. *One amusing new game is called Gossip Five. People are divided into two teams. Each team member writes down the name of five people whom he or she knows are remotely acquainted with the others present. The names are then put into a cap and withdrawn five at a time and pinned on to a blackboard. The teams are given five minutes to work in silence, writing down a little-known fact or piece of gossip about each of the names on the board. The team leader then collates the information and reads out the best or newest piece of gossip for each person. Teams are awarded five points for each new piece of gossip and no points for gossip that everyone knew already. Each member of the losing team is then required to give five pounds to each member of the winning team.*

INSTRUCTIONS FOR HOUSE PARTY GUESTS

Persons invited to spend time as members of a house party must consider themselves fortunate. There is no more fertile ground for the recruitment of potential new friends or romantic partners. The quasi-domestic scenario affords a unique opportunity to develop relationships which will remain associated in the mind with relaxation and enjoyment. What is more, the continuous and intimate exposure to fellow guests means that artificiality of behaviour is made redundant. A friendship forged at a house party will therefore be fond, ful-filling and long-lasting, unlike, for example, a friendship formed in a nightclub which can be based on misleading projec-tions of personality.

In budgetary terms, a house party holiday is equally attrac-tive. The cost of tipping and travelling must of course be taken into account but the only other necessary outlay will be a small present for the hostess and/or a minimal contribution to the cost of the fayre provided.

In the current economic climate, contributions towards the cost of catering are welcomed by many hostesses, even those who rank amongst the grandest. To calculate what amount, if any, would be appropriate, guests need simply draw their hos-tess aside shortly after their arrival and, in a casual manner, say brightly, but firmly, 'I'm going into (the nearest town with a

Waitrose or similar). What would you like as a contribution? I'm extremely happy to make one.'

At this point your hostess will reply, 'Absolutely not. You're our guest', in which case you may climb down. Or, 'Are you sure? Well, it would be lovely if you could get a couple of bottles of red wine.' If she says, 'Are you sure? Well, we'd love some red wine,' then you should buy a crate.

Bear in mind that even with such a contribution worth, say £50, for a crate of middle-quality wine, you will still be recouping all your total outlay as you can expect to ingest food and drink to the value of over and above this amount. When you also take into consideration the cost of nightclubs, restaurants and taxis which you would normally have to pay to involve yourself in a social scenario, then you will see such a contribution as a sensible one as it may ensure that you are invited again.

INSECURITIES OVER TIPPING

Q. I have been invited to stay at Blenheim for the weekend of 15-17 April. I am very embarrassed about the whole business of tipping and wonder whom, as a single female, I will be expected to tip and how much?   B.St G., Edinburgh

A. *As a single girl you would be expected to leave £10 in your bedroom or possibly £15 if the staff have done a lot for you. Do not make the mistake, as one visitor recently did at a similar stately home, of presuming that, as her case had been packed for her, the staff had also taken the initiative of removing the requisite amount from her purse.*

AIDS TO THE REDUCTION OF EMBARRASSMENT DURING AFTER-DINNER PLAYS

Q. My boyfriend and I have been invited to spend Easter in a really beautiful house in Pembrokeshire along with twenty other people. Instead of being really excited, I am dreading it. My boyfriend wants to be a playwright and he has written a one-man show which he is going to perform after dinner one night in front of everyone. The script is actually very funny, but the people who will be staying are all rather screwed up and conventional and bound not to laugh, but just be really embarrassed. I am sure this will stunt

Andrew's confidence and be a major setback to him. What can I do, as he is determined to go ahead with it and now our hostess has told everyone that he will be doing it? J.F., Cranmer Court, S.W.3

A. *Tapes are available from the BBC Sound Effects Library, among them a pre-recorded laughter cassette in which audiences of up to 300 people can be heard laughing. Use this tape to accompany your boyfriend's performance, operating the stop-start button when appropriate. His audience will be carried along, whether or not they think the play is in itself amusing. The lasting impression will be one of hilarity and equally should serve to boost your boyfriend's confidence to a considerable degree.*

A SUITABLE HOUSEPARTY GIFT FOR A HOSTESS WHO HAS EVERYTHING

Q. I have been invited to stay for a weekend in a certain country house to which it would be ludicrous to bring a gift of wine or flowers. What does one bring to a house with a famous garden and wine cellar? Chocolates are equally unsuitable as the cook makes his own.   N.C., S.W.10

A. *Why not present your hostess with a sheet of one hundred first-class stamps? For people who do not have access to office postroom facilities, queuing in post offices constitutes a major irritant. Your gift will have long-term reverberations as your hostess will associate you with pleasure every time she posts a letter in the weeks that follow your visit.*

FAILURE TO HAVE WRITTEN A THANK YOU LETTER

Q. I am deeply embarrassed by an oversight I have recently committed. A close neighbour, to whom I am rather keen to suck up, invited my husband and me to spend some days shooting at her house in Yorkshire. We went and had a spectacularly good time (although there was too big a bag) – food, drink, fires in the bedrooms, staff outnumbering the guests – everything was perfect. I did mean to write and thank, but we all travelled down together in the plane, and then by car from the airport to our village and then we saw one another the very next morning. I frankly didn't get round to it. In truth it somehow seemed rather artificial to write when one had verbally expressed what a wonderful time one had had, almost ad nauseam, during the return journey. Plus I would have had to deliver the letter personally as it would have been ludicrous to post it when we live within ninety seconds', walk of each other. I am sorry to bang on for so long, but the point is, my neighbour's attitude towards me has undergone a perceptible change and I am sure it is to do with my not having written. It is now far too late. What can I do?　　H.S., Ludgershall

A. *Write the thank-you letter you would have written, had you got down to it, on the day of your return from the shooting holiday. Date it as such. Enclose within it a pair of Thomas Pink cufflinks explaining that you have found these amongst your own luggage but they do not belong to you. Put the lot in an envelope and seal it up. Then put the slim package under a doormat in the entrance hall to your own accommodation and 'grossle' the mat round and round on top to effect an aged appearance. Next, conceal the letter about your person and make the ninety-second journey to your neighbour's house. Make a stealthy approach. Once you have gained admission through her own entrance hall, pop the letter under her doormat. 'Hello,' you can say, 'I just popped in to say that those Thomas Pink cufflinks belong to (your husbands name) after all.'*

'What Thomas Pink cufflinks?' she will reply, mystified. At this stage a hunt for the letter which you 'pushed under the door the day after we got back', may ensue.

Crackling fires, drinks twice daily and group jigsaws usually ensure low tension in a house party. However, after-dinner performances are fertile sources of embarrassment.

How should one best alert someone who has been dancing reels for fifteen minutes that their skirt is tucked into their tights?

Dance Parties

Hosting a Dance

THE CORRECT PROCEDURE FOR hosting a successful dance party involves the recruitment of one's most 'trendy' dancing friends to act in advisory capacities. It is they who can inform a hostess most reliably when when she is selecting the music, which is of paramount importance to such events.

What the music must do is to make the people who make the party want to dance. It is the so-called Hard Core, who are excited by good music, who set the tone and atmosphere of a party. Their approval will be manifested by whether or not they take to the floor with enthusiasm. If they do, their electric spirit will create a ripple effect throughout the party.

'Forget spending the money on the drink and the food,' says one experienced hostess, 'Spend the money on the music. It must be either Lester Lanin or a non-stop band that can give constantly good music.' But the important thing is that both live and pre-recorded music be selected with the advice of the aforementioned rhythmically proficient dancing friends.

Inability to Dance Properly

Q. I always dread dances because, for a variety of reasons, I am a rather inhibited and bad dancer. I feel being a bad dancer is incredibly damaging to one's image as people always think it means that one is no good in bed and I have a recurring waking nightmare in which people surround me on the dance floor, as they do in Fred Astaire and Ginger Rogers films, but instead of clapping to an approving beat, they are nodding knowingly at one another and making their own conclusions as they watch me move clumsily and unrhythmically about the floor. What can I do? There is no point in advising dancing lessons because it is the free expression modern style of dancing which is my problem.

J.L., near Dublin

A. *Many successful socialisers in your position have adopted the following method to disguise their inadequacy. Take up*

15

your position on the floor with assurance, pushing through the crowd towards your selected performance area with an expression of excited anticipation.

Having arrived there you should launch into a series of seemingly involuntary spasms which are so very greatly out of time with the music that there can be no question that you are unable to keep up with it. The confidence of your convulsions rather implies that, on the contrary, you are dancing with greater skill than the others who surround you. Many of those who choose this method can gauge the approval of adjoining dancers by observing their involuntary mimicking.

At the very worst your dancing will be interpreted as merely eccentric and there should be no means at all for your fellow dancers to discover that you are no good in bed.

FOOD AND DRINK AT A DANCE

It is not always necessary to serve champagne at a dance. In fact, you may even do your guests an unwitting disservice by offering it. Contrary to popular belief, champagne can actually be rather dispiriting, particularly if it is of low quality or supplies of it are curtailed after an initial abundance and guests must switch to wine, or worse, spirits.

Vintage champagne is, of course, another matter, and on the very rare occasions where a host can afford to supply his guests with an evening's worth, then he can be assured that an almost nirvana-like sense of well-being will pervade his guests throughout the entire evening.

A cocktail can be a successful alternative, but on no account should two types of spirits be mixed together to create one. This will bring on two-, even three-day hangovers in almost all who ingest such a concoction. And low-quality wine will have the same effect.

One popular cocktail which is both refreshing and invigorating is the underused 'Hunchback of Notre Dame', which consists of white rum, orange juice and grenadine.

BUFFET FOOD
Food should be chosen with care so that guests may continue to enjoy the relaxed, carefree mood that should have been engen-

dered by the correct choice of cocktail and wine. This will not be possible if there is any danger that dignity may be compromised during the ingestion of unwisely chosen foodstuffs.

Digito-buccal buffets are most sensibly offered to teenagers as they can then disguise the number of things they are putting into their mouths. When required to load their own plate at a buffet, they may be self-conscious about quantities.

Spare ribs should not be offered to guests under the age of twenty as such people are equally self-conscious about the obligatory method of ingestion. A more suitable alternative would be anything served in nugget form, such as fish balls or spinach and cheese balls in a breadcrumb coating. These can easily be conveyed to the mouth. Needless to say, nothing *soppresso*, with which jets of garlic or other juices can be released over the facial area during consumption, should be served.

Fully grown and self-confident adults, on the other hand, will often revel in the novelty of eating food from a hot dog van, or a fish and chip van especially hired for the occasion. These are particularly suitable for country parties which are often held in barns or marques in any case.

Somewhere proper to sit and somewhere proper to stand are essential, as are adequate surfaces. The unsatisfactoriness of consuming food and drink without sufficient surfaces on which to 'rest' them between mouthfuls can be likened to being tickled with one's clothes on. And of course you will want your guests to derive the maximum pleasure possible.

FORMAL FOOD
Formal sit-down dinners tend to prompt one particular problem.

FORCING PEOPLE TO SIT DOWN FOR DINNER

Q. How can I make people sit down for dinner at my forthcoming thirtieth birthday dance? At my sister's thirtieth the food was ruined because people simply wouldn't stop talking and sit down.   S.L., S.W.3

A. *A microphone should initially be employed to instruct guests to make their way to the tables ten full minutes before you actually wish them to do so. Following this announcement, all replenishing of drinks should be halted and tray-*

bearing waiters should begin to circulate forcefully through the throng saying, 'May I take your glass, Sir (or Madam)?' Most guests will find that standing up talking without a drink is less agreeable than with. It should therefore be less than ten minutes before they take the decision to move towards their positions at a table where they can find further refreshment.

TRIGGER LISTS

Occasionally it does slip people's minds that certain other people are actually their friends and they *genuinely* forget to invite them to parties. For easy reference purposes a trigger list can be used to remind oneself of who ought to be asked.

A trigger list can be run up in a couple of hours by any competent typist. The party-giver simply goes through her address book and dictates names only of all living friends to the typist who types the names in columnar form. She then reduces the list on a photocopy machine, to playing card size, whereupon it can be sent to a laminating company.

You will find this device invaluable when you are compiling guest lists because you can easily refer to it while lolling on a sofa with a third party standing by to take dictation. You can update this as and when you require it, depending on how often you make new friends.

It may well be necessary to invite certain people who you actually dislike to your party. Some people are driven to planning parties around the dates that certain others will be out of the country so that they can have the credit for asking them but can be reassured that they will be unable to come. Yet one can still see large groups of guests at any party who are disliked by the person who has found herself obliged to invite them. This is an unavoidable aspect of sophisticated society

JOGGING THE MEMORY OF A HOSTESS WHO HAS FAILED TO INVITE A MUTUAL FRIEND OF YOURS TO A DANCE

Q. The invitations have started to arrive for a rather spectacular dance which is being held at B*******, very near to where I live in the country, next month. A great friend of mine is desperately keen to go and believes that the person giving the dance is very vague and has therefore just forgotten to invite her. How can I jog her memory? I feel I cannot simply ask directly, 'Are you inviting Isabella?', but must skirt around it somehow so that, should she wish not to invite Isabella, she need not say so directly to me.

K.F., Watlington

A. *You can telephone the hostess and say, 'Thank you for the invitation. I would love to come. Can I put anyone up? What mutual friends have you invited?' In this way you offer her the opportunity to say, 'Well, I have asked Isabella, Hugo and Gerry', for example, or to make it clear by her failure to mention their names that they have not been invited.*

A Dignified way of Gate-Crashing a Dance

Q. I have so far failed to receive an invitation to the dance at A. later this month. It is ridiculous because I know of at least three other people who hardly know E and G who have been asked and I have known them both for years on and off. Do you think I should just ring up and demand one? The invitation reads 'Please bring this card with you'; otherwise I would just crash it.

A.Z., S.W.10

A. *Such a move would be undignified. Far better to write a traditional card of acceptance to the dance, enclosing a note which reads, 'Please could you send me another invitation card to the dance as I cannot find mine.'*

Dress Tucked into Tights

Q. What is the correct protocol for alerting someone that they have been dancing reels for a full fifteen minutes with their dress tucked into their tights at the back? The incident I witnessed occurred at the Northern Meeting and involved a rather formidable fifty-year-old local dignitary of my acquaintance who had just emerged from the ladies cloakroom before taking the floor and was obviously slightly the worse for wear. Although the spectacle was exceedingly enjoyable to watch, I felt it was rather *lese majeste* and that I, or someone, should have done something. Yet, as you can

19

imagine, no one could bring themselves to tell her. What should we have done?   A.St C., The Black Isle

A. *As many of those men present would have undoubtedly been wearing skean-dhus, it should have been relatively easy for one of them to put this dagger-like instrument to effective use by discreetly slashing the elastic at the waist-band of the tights worn by the lady in question while engaging her in seated conversation. In this way the skirts of the dress would have been swiftly returned to floor level.*

How pompous and fogey is it exactly to expect women to leave the dinner table
while men continue to drink port?

DINNER PARTIES

HOSTING DINNER PARTIES

DINNER PARTIES ARE PIVOTAL to the promotion of one's personal prestige. Hosts should realise, however, that displays of wealth, taste and status-rich friends are not key factors in the success of such an occasion. Indeed, they may even induce resentment amongst competitive guests.

The key ingredient in the recipe for a successful dinner party is the induction of a slow and insidious sensation in the minds of guests that their own personal prestige has somehow been promoted. This sensation may be brought about by a variety of means.

It is of primary importance that guests feel themselves to be physically attractive during the course of the evening. To this purpose antique glass should be used in all reception rooms. Alternatively, full-length 'slimming' mirrors as used by the more corrupt fashion retailers can be purchased from T & W Ide of Stepney in London's East End (081 790 2333). As a tertiary measure there should be a proliferation of candles rather than artificial lighting as this will disguise defects in the skin tones of those present. Naturally each guest should be complimented on his or her appearance on arrival. Do not use the adjective 'amazing', however; its ambiguity can be unsettling to those who lack confidence.

The correct ambience may be set in motion by the use of crackling fires. Flames have an hypnotic effect which is useful in reducing tension and the crackling can also serve to mask pauses in conversation. Some log-effect fires now come with enhanced roaring which can be equally effective. Barbecues can play the same role.

A stiff champagne, vodka or whisky-based cocktail must be served to induce a temporary euphoria at the start of the evening. Wine is too lulling to begin with.

CONVERSATION

Self-confidence and uninhibitedness thus bolstered, guests

should be ready to take part in sparkling conversations during the pre-dinner period. On no account, however, should one guest be allowed to dominate the conversation at this stage. If you make the serious mistake of seating people in one block – for example, on a pair of facing sofas, or even at the dinner table before dinner has been served – you will find that whoever starts talking will feel himself obliged to address everyone present, making laborious eye contact by rote.

His captive audience, meanwhile, will be impatiently 'queuing' to talk themselves, despite their grinning appreciation of the monologue. Group them in mini-clusters, therefore, to preclude this possibility.

STIMULATORS

Q. We often hear of conversation-killers, but have you any suggestions for conversation-starters to be used when one is giving a dinner party? Many of my friends are frightfully dull.   A.W., Callow Street, S.W.3

A. *Ideally, a mini-drama of some kind will get the evening off to a good start and produce animated discussion – a raid by the police, for example, following an 'anonymous' tip-off that Lord Lucan is present at the dinner party would be ideal were it not impractical, as one does then run the risk of serving a sentence for wasting police time.*

Some sort of small domestic catastrophe will always put guests at their ease. Power cuts are popular as they are inexpensive and easy to effect. If a good deal of stickiness is anticipated, this can even be staged to coincide with the arrival of a Kissogram girl or boy who has been instructed to make passes at those guests whose confidence needs to be particularly boosted or who would otherwise have little conversation during the evening. When the power has been restored (an additional opportunity for morale-boosting is offered here for the person who understands tripswitches), you can then show out the intruder, pretending you are outraged by this practical joke someone has obviously played on you.

PLACEMENT

Spontaneous placement is rarely as effective as controlled

placement. Places should be firmly labelled and hosts should be on their guard against anarchic disruption of their scheme. You should hint to each guest that at least one of the people on either their left or their right fancies them. Flattered, but secure in the knowledge that no pass can be made at the table, a potent degree of flirting should then be set in motion.

TURNING

Q. I was absolutely set upon by someone the other night for not turning. It was not even his dinner so I don't quite know why he was so agitated about it. What is the correct protocol incidentally? H.P., Andover

A. *A woman is expected to talk throughout the first course to the man on her left and turn for the second course to the man on her right. Vice-versa for men, of course. However the system is faintly pompous and pretentious unless one is dining in an embassy or at Buck House.*

POMPOSITY

Q. How pompous and fogey is it exactly to require women to leave the table and go upstairs while men continue to drink port? I say very, but my twenty-eight-year-old boyfriend, who is desirable in every other respect, has indicated that he expects me to lead the women out when we give dinners together at his house in Thurloe Square. So far I have refused. What is your view? K.St B.M., S.W.7

A. *Why not make a feature of his fogeydom? Though the custom is pompous, most women nonetheless welcome the chance to lie flat on their backs in unattractive poses, after the sort of stupifyingly heavy dinner which fogeys tend to favour. They also enjoy poking around another person's bedroom and going to the loo. And all this while the men are still sitting uncomfortably at table making themselves seriously ill. A port hangover tends to start as one is drinking it.*

FOOD POISONING

Q. How should one apologise to people whom one has

poisoned? We recently gave lunch to thirty girls who were at school with our daughter and rather meanly used the caterer who had given us the cheapest quote. Chicken was served and everyone seemed very happy, but in a straw poll I conducted six girls out of ten seem to have gone down with some sort of mild food poisoning. Should we write to each girl individually and apologise?   C.B., Honington

A. *It should not be necessary. Most young girls are only too pleased to suffer from minor digestive disorders from time to time as it enables them to lose weight.*

ATTENDING DINNER PARTIES

NOISY EATING

Far too many people are under the erroneous assumption that soup should be introduced to the mouth through suction rather than tipping. Other common annoyances are clanking of the fork against the china as each mouthful is loaded, and clattering during the taking-away period. These noises are fantastically irritating to many people and nerves can be jangled irreparably for the full evening by any one of them.

Q. How can I stop my husband from slurping soup and coffee? He simply does not believe that anyone except me minds and that I only mind because I am 'half mad'.

M.K., Marlborough

A. *If he already thinks you are half mad then there can be no harm in your starting a petition. Head it, 'We, the undersigned, find slurping unattractive'. You should have no difficulty in amassing sufficient signatories from amongst your acquaintances in a short period to provide written proof of slurping's offensiveness.*

EXPULSION OF PERSONAL GASES DURING DINNER

Q. I am soon to attend a smart dinner party of a successful magazine editor here in New York. I have learned in advance that my hostess is planning to serve a traditional Indian meal in honour of a fellow guest. My problem is this: I fear an embarrassing situation may arise as I know I am prone to pass wind on the consumption of spice-laden foods. A friend has suggested the insertion of a small cushion inside the seat of my trousers in order that any unpleasant sounds may be drowned out. This seems to me an inconvenient and uncomfortable solution. What do you advise?

V.D., Greene Street, N.Y. 10012

A. *Charcoal tablets, available at any chemist at small cost, will soak up intestinal wind. These, however, can leave a black powdery coating on the lips. Why not take lots to the party and pass them round as an 'ethnic' accompaniment to the meal? Alternatively, you may insist upon bringing a small dog and blame any untoward sounds on the pooch.*

THE INCORRECT CLOTHING

Q. I turned up to a dinner at someone's house the other night and found that everyone else was in black tie. It was too late to go home and change. What should I have done?

A.G., Isle of Dogs

A. *Invalids are excused full evening dress so, in collusion with your host, you should have barged through to the bedroom before taking off your coat, and borrowed a dressing gown to substitute for your jacket. You could then have appeared at dinner apologising for being incorrectly dressed but explaining that you were ill and only allowed out of bed for a few hours.*

BRINGING A BOTTLE

The custom of bringing a bottle was prevalent in the 1970s and early 1980s but in recent days the matter has caused anxiety to hosts and guests alike. If your host is, say, Sir James Goldsmith or the Duchess of Westminster, then wine would be an inappropriate gift. However, when invited by middle-income group hosts to a house you have not previously visited, it is advisable to bring one goodish bottle for each member of your party (not more than three). Carry these in a large dark bag and produce them if it seems they would be eagerly received. While some prefer to demonstrate their largesse and genuinely do not want a contribution from guests, others feel that as the cost of an even moderate lunch party for four runs to an average of £60, then they are anxious to recoup part of their outlay as quickly as possible.

Q. How can one ensure that, having brought some very good

wine to a dinner party, the host does not say 'Oh thank you', and put it in a cupboard while serving you Bulgarian Cabernet, or worse, a vinegary Muscadet. I come from a family of wine-importers and my palate is perhaps more sensitive than those of other people   R.R., S.W.10

A. *Bring only red wine. Then you can say, 'This needs to be opened now, to breathe', as you hand it over. In extreme circumstances you can bring a full, though uncorked, bottle and on presentation say, 'This has been breathing at home'. Alternatively, bring a bottle of chilled champagne which will obviously require immediate consumption.*

WHEN TO ARRIVE

Q. I was terribly embarrassed the other night to have arrived too early for dinner. As soon as my host opened the door I could tell by the look on his face that he was not expecting me for at least half an hour. It meant that he was 'faffing around' with his last-minute preparations at the same time as trying to entertain me. He was in the most frightfully irritable state. What should I have done? He refused my offers of assistance.   M.M., Honiton

A. *People who suspect they may have arrived prematurely for a dinner engagement should be prepared to address the door-opener with the following bright enquiry, 'Oh hello. I just called to ask you what time dinner was before I go for my stroll'. You can then temper your stroll to fit the length of time of the interval between your enquiry and the commencement of dinner.*

WHO ELSE IS COMING?

Q. I know it is terribly rude to ask 'Who else is coming?' before accepting an invitation to dinner, but with certain hostesses one really does run the risk of being faced with a line-up of dullards. How can one ascertain this knowledge before agreeing to attend, and without giving offence? B.F., W.11

A. *You should telephone your hostess thanking her for the invitation but should state solemnly, 'I'm going to have to ask you who else is coming before I say yes or no. I'll explain why in a moment'.*

If the roll call is promising, you can hurriedly interject,

'Stop right there. I've been exposed to German measles, but I'm just looking at my medical handbook and I'm past the stage of being a danger to pregnant women'. If, on the other hand, you decide you do not wish to be one of the number, you can say, 'Much as I'd love to see you I don't think it would be a good idea. I have a large suppurating cyst in the centre of my forehead at the moment and I really don't feel I could face seeing anyone who isn't a very old friend – and I'm quite sure they couldn't face seeing me'.

DRINKS PARTIES

PEOPLE ALMOST ALWAYS ENJOY drinks parties for the simple reason that they take up so little time. Whether they are held between 7.00 and 9.00 or, as often happens in London, do not even begin until 10.30 p.m., it would be churlish to complain. After all, one is at liberty to do what one wants with the rest of the evening, even if the drinks party itself is 'awful'.

Yet how 'awful' can a drinks party be when it will almost certainly offer one the means to work off a number of one's friends and/or the chance to build up new social and work contacts for the purposes of general advancement? And all this entirely free of charge. It may also offer the opportunity to interact with people that one either wishes merely to flirt with, or even actually to 'get off' with.

Hostesses who are already established in complacent couple-dom should not forget the essential social service that they can perform by hosting a drinks party to which they invite a sizeable number of singles. It is a less obvious, yet far, far more charitable thing that they do then, than for example, attending a lunch costing £175 which may benefit a straightforward charity such as the AIDS Crisis Trust or Birthright.

Why, for £175 one can buy seventeen bottles of champagne and invite thirty-four people to drink it, or fifty bottles of drinkable wine and invite one hundred people to drink it.

Even if only two of those invited become romantically attached to one another, a great good will have been indirectly done. To supply another person with a romantic partner is one of the greatest favours one can do him or her, though naturally a hostess should avoid being heavy-handed about forcing obvious spinsters and bachelors into conversational clusters.

Drinks parties can provide a social service of almost equal worth by introducing people who simply become friends. For those who are suffering from friend fatigue, it is a common and selfish mistake to presume that the appetites of others are equally jaded. They forget the early days of friendship recruitment when they spent hour after hour and night after night alone, aching inside for want of company. Now that they have rounded up all the friends they can possibly service, and the ring of a telephone sets adrenalin rushing through their systems as they dread another invitation, they have forgotten the days when one drinks party would form the highlight of a whole month.

And where can the friend-hungry meet these new people who are roughly on the same wavelength as themselves? Certainly not through maundling around the Tate Gallery vaguely staring at the same painting and certainly not through evening classes. No, it is the direct duty of a woman of social conscience to throw parties as regularly as she can afford them so that the socially impoverished can meet one another and thereby enrich their lifestyles.

The additional social service offered by a drinks party is that one is given the excuse to further relationships with flimsy acquaintances by saying, 'Would you like to have dinner after so and so's drinks party?'

PLANNING A DRINKS PARTY

Top caterer and butler-trainer Martin Buckeridge used always to say that a good hostess never enjoys her own party until after it has happened.

That is correct. If a hostess enjoyed her drinks party while it was happening it would mean that she was not on full alert to ensure that the correct introductions were being made. Delicately, of course – guests do not like to think they are being manipulated. She may not enjoy the evening but she will enjoy its repercussions.

WHO TO INVITE (THE VIEILLESSE DORÉE)

Invite more people than you can fit into the room rather than less. Invite as many very old people as you can – especially gay old men who like talking about sex in an amusing way. There is currently a vogue for members of what might be called the Vieillesse Dorée, which are people born before 1930.

Just as being young was once *de rigeur,* the extremely old now have the upper hand in terms of social desirability. This is partly because their characters and intellects were developed in the days before media pollution, when brains were active questors rather than passive receptors. Consequently their conversation tends to be of above-average calibre.

Apparently there used also to be fixed moral codes from which one could deviate, if one wanted, and then feel guilty or thrilled. Thrills were thrilling in those days and such people, whose lives were 'real', have a lot to offer those born after 1960, to whom champagne, sophisticated gourmet dishes and casual sex are on tap seven days a week. But younger guests should be briefed about tactfulness.

TACTLESSNESS WITH THE VIEILLESSE DORÉE

Q. I am having what you might describe as a 'Dodder on Down' drinks party for my grandfather's birthday. At least half of the people I am inviting are over sixty, and the other half are all around twenty-two – my own age group. Are there any specific tips you might offer me for making the evening between these disparate groups go well? Can one hire megaphones in bulk, for example?   M.W.D., S.W.1

A. *Many people of over sixty are rather spry these days and need not be treated as though they are attending their last party. It should be unnecessary to hire megaphones unless you intend to play loud music as accompaniment. Many people of twenty-two feel that a drinks party provides a unique opportunity to make a statement of identity to their guests as to their own musical tastes. However, not to play such music is a sacrifice that will be sensibly made, as your grandfather's friends will no doubt find modern music an irritant.*

Apart from this, and providing adequate seating, you may proceed as you would for an ordinary drinks party. Do, however, brief those among your friends who are inclined to be tactless so that they do not fall into the trap of addressing questions such as 'Who was the most interesting person you ever met?' or 'What was the most exciting thing that ever happened to you?', as though the life of their interlocutor were moving to a close that very evening.

May I add that, the older certain people are, the more likely it is that they live in accommodation which is rather attractive and conveniently situated – especially if they are social figures. For this reason you can do some of your more

impoverished friends a favour by inviting them along. Some
of the fogies may well have spare rooms in their flats or
houses which they are only too happy to fill with young
people, charging them only a peppercorn rent.

See also the chapter entitled Social Infiltration (page 40).

COPING WITH A LEG IN PLASTER AT A DRINKS PARTY

Q. I have recently broken my leg and it will be in plaster for
some months. I am still capable of attending parties though
I obviously have to remain seated throughout. Can you suggest a way in which I can encourage bores to move on as I am
something of a sitting target at such events?   M.S., W.2

A. *Conceal a spare glass about your person as you take up your*
semi-recumbent position. If and when you wish to clear the
space next to you to make way for an alternative inter-
locutor, simply produce the empty glass and ask that it be
refilled by the person beside you. With any luck his seat will
also have been refilled on his return. You may then dis-
creetly tip the contents of the 'refilled' glass into the one you
are already drinking, thus releasing another empty glass for
the same purpose as the party proceeds.

HAND-SHAKING

In recent years confusion has reigned in social circles over
when and where the gesture of hand-shaking is appropriate.
World travel, the advent of double kissing, the relaxation and
then reintroduction of traditional modes of behaviour – all
these factors have served to make hazy the expectations of in-
troducees in every presentation bar the most formal (royal
family, etc.).

Shooting and hunting introductions are minefields of potential disconcertion. Many 'guns' only tip their hats lightly on introductions. If someone is unfamiliar with the custom, the gun-
man must reply to their proffered paw and many accidental
bursts of gunfire are discharged in the process.

In riding circles the hard hat is removed in a rainbow-shaped
sweeping gesture and replaced while those on the ground nod

back. Many of those new to horseplay are unaware of this protocol and hands will be extended. Though mounted riders will
not generally fall from their horses in trying to respond, the
business is an ungainly one.

At drinks parties, however, the hand-shaking problem is at
its most visible.

Q. I wish to avoid the embarrassment of putting out my hand to
shake someone else's, on introduction, and then finding
that they have not extended their own. I do not always ex-
tend my hand as a matter of course. In fact, sometimes I
deliberately withhold it because I suspect that the other
person is not expecting it. Then they do offer theirs and I
belatedly produce my own with a compensatory overlarge
grin. I find this aspect of drinks parties most embarrassing.
What do you advise?   P.M., W.8

A. *When introductions are likely to be made, it is advisable to
engage the forearm in a permanent semi-slack projection.
A handbag or cellular telephone hung over the arm will
give validity to this gesture, though it can easily pass for
affectation. Staring into the eyes of your fellow introducee,
you may either grip their hand positively if it comes forward, or maintain your outstretched hand gesture without
embarrassment.*

How to get away from People at a Drinks Party

Q. How can I move on at a drinks party without appearing to
be rude?   M.G.C., Inverness

A. *Gradually and imperceptibly allow the space between you
and your interlocutor to become larger. Meantime allow a
vague expression to pass over your face. Soon others will
start to push through the gap, assuming it is a passageway.
Having lost contact, it should be easy for you to slip away.*

*Alternatively, on greeting each interlocutor, state that
you are worried about your car which you have parked
badly. After a while you can easily say, 'I must go and check
my car'.*

DISGUISING ONE'S HUSBAND'S INTELLECTUAL INADEQUACY AT A DRINKS PARTY

Q. Is there any way of disguising the intellectual inadequacy of one's husband? I am soon to take up a position at an Oxford college and will be required to attend certain drinks parties with my husband in tow. I have asked him to pretend to have laryngitis on these occasions, but he became rather pugnacious at this suggestion. What should I do?

M.W., Bolton

A. *Why not simply sprinkle his clothes with a small measure of whisky before leaving for these occasions so that a strong smell of alcohol pervades his presence? It is likely that his stupidity will then be mistaken for drunkenness.*

INTRODUCING PEOPLE WHOSE NAMES YOU HAVE FORGOTTEN

Q. I dread going to drinks parties as I often forget people's names and find myself at a loss when obliged to introduce them to a third party. What is the best way to deal with such a problem without offending the person whose name one has forgotten?

S.M., Littleton Panel

A. *When you sense the approach of a third party it is sensible to say to the person whose name you have forgotten, 'You'll have to introduce yourself. I always get very flustered at parties'. Alternatively you can mumble the 'name' of the unknown person so that the third party can say 'I'm sorry, I didn't catch your name'.*

A NOVEL WAY OF MAKING A DRINKS PARTY GO WITH A SWING

Q. I am shortly to give a drinks party for some rather shy teenagers. Can you suggest a means by which I can make the party go with a swing?

P.T., Lincs

A. *Many teenagers enjoy structure as it serves to avoid the embarrassment of approaching people they 'like' without due reason. Therefore you should hold the party in a room*

*where the floor may be masking-taped with numbers. You
then issue cards, rather like dance cards, so that the guests
should take up, say, ten different positions of ten minutes
each, changeable at the ring of a bell. This way they will
each talk to ten different people. You will find that many
shy teenagers find this a most exciting way of conducting an
evening.*

How to get away from other People who are trying to join your Dinner Party after the Drinks Party

Q. One thing I find difficult about drinks parties is that, when
one has rounded up a congenial set of people to have dinner
with afterwards, other people come up and say, 'What are
you doing after this?' How do you stop them from coming
too?   M.S., S.W.1

A. *You should put the ball in another person's court. Think
carefully about who might be present who might be both
outside your interlocutor's range of social reference and
also might be even intimidating to him. say, 'Hugh (for
example) has booked a table somewhere. I'm going with
him.' The following day on the telephone you can report
back that Hugh himself 'never showed up at the
restaurant'.*

Dealing with People who fail to bring a Bottle to a Bring-A-Bottle Party

Q. I am a student in my second year at Durham University.
The problem of this particular university is that, while some
of the students have hefty private incomes, the rest of us are
on grants. Paradoxically, it is the richest students who often
turn up at a bring-a-bottle party without a bottle. It is not so
much because they are mean, though I am well aware that
the rich are traditionally much meaner than the poor, but
that they are not really accustomed to bringing bottles to
drinks parties and so they tend to forget they are supposed
to bring one and turn up without. This means that the in-
iquitous situation arises whereby the poor students are sub-

sidising the social pleasures of the rich. I do not mind myself, as I personally have attended drinks parties given by these same people where I did not have to bring a bottle, but my other friends, who will not receive hospitality at a later date, do resent it. What should we do about it?

P.J., Durham

A. *Why not adopt the bring-a-bottle party method which was used with success by fashionable surveyor Philip Wood when he was a student at Durham in the late 1980s.*

Wood termed his parties 'Buy-a-bottle' rather than 'Bring-a-bottle' and typical invitations would read: 'Philip Wood invites you to a Buy-a-bottle party on Saturday 21st May in H14, the Castle. Bulgarian Cabernet Sauvignon and Eden beer will be sold on site'.

Wood himself would 'front' the money for the Eden and Cabernet Sauvignon which he ordered on sale or return from a local off-licence at a quota allowing one bottle per head. On arrival guests would hand over the sum of around £2 and be given their own bottle of either wine or Eden in exchange. Although the students were initially inclined to grumble that they were being 'ripped off' by Wood, they swiftly realised how much more satisfactory an arrangement it was – not only in terms of fairness but also in terms of convenience and of physical fitness. No longer need they consume a disabling hotch-potch of low-level alcoholic poisons but could stick to the same, acceptable quality (as Bulgarian Cabernet was in those days) for the full evening.

HOW TO GET RID OF PEOPLE AT THE END OF A DRINKS PARTY

Q. I love giving drinks parties, with one reservation. I like to collapse afterwards but I find that certain of one's friends and contacts will always stay on well beyond the time stipulated for departure on their invitation. These are generally people who have been inefficient about making arrangements for dinner and so are left at something of a loose end when everyone else goes off.

They then stay on, spinning out the rest of the evening by eating crisps and peanuts. Then one hears them ask, 'You haven't got a slice of bread I could have?' rather accusingly.

How can one effect the departure of late-staying guests?

B.R., Eaton Place

A. *Although you say you like to collapse after such an occasion, many hostesses in your position would be expected to go out to dinner themselves. Therefore, at a moment when you are satisfied that enough has been enough, you should put on your coat and tell those guests who are remaining: 'I've got a dinner date, but do please stay on. The only thing is that, if you are going to stay on, then I must give someone the responsibility of turning off the burglar alarm, so who is going to be the last person to leave, because that would be the most sensible person to do it?'*

You will find that the late-stayers will rise, as a man, from their trays of peanuts, saying, 'Oh, it won't be me. I must go now'.

Hostesses may note, as a general rule, that it is unwise to allow their waiters to be overtly attentive during a drinks party. Many socialisers will be relying on the old device of 'getting another drink' to enable them to get away from people without being rude. Why, even with one's oldest friends who know how much one adores them, one does not like to say 'All right, let's split up now and go and talk to some new people.'

Getting away from work colleagues at a drinks party can be even more difficult. The artificiality of the friendship one generally has with a work colleague means that one tends to overcompensate at social events by remaining glued to the side of this person.

Therefore, though waiters should be on hand, if one can afford them, to dispense drinks from behind a table, it is imperative that they should not circulate through the crowd except in special circumstances.

What is the correct sound to emit when kissing a friend by way of greeting or departure?

SOCIAL INFILTRATION

THE CONCEPT OF SOCIAL climbing is unattractive. It suggests that it is possible for a person who does not merit the affections or interest of certain others of supposedly higher rank or superior intelligence to inveigle a dodgy inclusion into their social schedule. The expression social climbing is therefore oxymoronic, as anyone who appears to be acceptable to any other person in a friendship capacity cannot therefore be reasonably said to have climbed.

Social infiltration, on the other hand, may well be of interest to readers of this book, and in this chapter we will discuss breaking into sets into which one is not automatically embosomed through reasons of work, birth or being a member of an educational community.

Just as marriage can be said to be to do with safety and recognition, and therefore one marries the girl next door or the girl at the next factory bench, so friendships are most easily formed through prolonged and natural exposure. It is all very well meeting people three times at drinks parties and talking to them with animation and rapport on each occasion, but a solid friendship will more easily be formed through spontaneous meetings, to which tension does not attach, such as being a house party guest or through work exposure. One needs an 'alibi' for seeing people or it may seem that too much hangs on the success of each encounter.

Everyone has their own idea of which set they wish to infiltrate and even formidable figures at the very top of the social and financial ladders are actively concerned with infiltration into other sets than their own. Usually such people wish to break into artistic, intellectual or professional sporting circles.

So whether one wishes to infiltrate the Sir James Goldsmith set, the Neil Kinnock set, the Julian and Isabel Bannerman set or the Brian Eno set, single encounters, even a series of them, will not necessarily help – unless one's character is of mesmerising and Rasputin-like compulsion. Friendship is to do with shared experiences and references; take the example of old schoolfriends – no matter how deeply two schoolfriends loved each other at the time, ten years later there may be nothing to talk about except the past.

GENERAL INSTRUCTIONS

Q. I wish I received more invitations. I am perfectly attractive and interesting but I don't seem to get invited out very often. What should I do about it?   C.S., S.W.10

A. *If you wish to increase the volume of your invitations (even if only for the purposes of reassurance), then you have to work at receiving them. Keep your answerphone on at all times, return people's calls, question them about their social activities in a manner which will give them the opportunity to invite you along if they should feel like it, keep friendships on the boil by ringing people to see how they are getting on. Do not presume, as many men do, that other people are mind readers and that they somehow know you are thinking about them.*

INFILTRATION HAVING MOVED HOUSE

Q. My husband and I have had to move from our rather smart house in Gloucestershire to somewhat humbler accommodation in Wiltshire. There are still plenty of 'our type' of people around but how are they going to realise that we are congenial? We have been asked to the local grandees' for drinks but I think they are simply being neighbourly. Name-dropping seems too crude a measure to adopt. What do you suggest?   R.St C., Pewsey

A. *Be noticeably reticent about your social contacts during the drinks but when you leave you should forget a small bag containing your filofax or address book. When you telephone later to arrange recovery you should find a marked increase in warmth in the local grandees' manner towards you.*

REPELLING UNWELCOME INFILTRATORS

Q. The most dreadful climber keeps ringing up wanting to be friends with me. She is always very oily and enquires after my well-being, etc., but she is obviously angling for an invitation. How can I put her off? I almost always end up by being embarrassed into asking her round.

D.V., Chippenham

A. *'What prompted you to call?' is always a very effective put-off line and has been used with success in discouraging all manner of relationships.*

DEFLECTING SUCKERS-UP

Q. Despite the fact that I have always tried to maintain a low profile, I was recently listed in a colour magazine article as being one of the richest people in this country. Although the article was widely off the mark in a great percentage of its inadequately researched assumptions, readers clearly perceived it to be factual. Since publication I have noted a marked increase in strangers making pleasant overtures towards me at parties. How can I sort out the wheat from the chaff? Anon, Bryanston Square, W.1

A. *Many millionaires recommend the inclusion of a false re-creation in their* Who's Who *entry as an ideal device to identify phoney would-be friends. One lists opera, which he 'cannot stand', and though he found it initially shocking to be approached by grinning strangers saying, 'I'm sure I saw you at the opera the other night', he now considers this an indispensable gauge of a stranger's intentions.*

SECURING AN INVITATION TO A DANCE

Q. I am absolutely desperately keen that I should be invited to a certain extremely smart dance which is being held on the 31st of this month. Though I have met the hostess through mutual friends, we do not have an independent relationship of our own. How do I best go about securing an invitation?

M.H., Smith Street, S.W.3

A. *The method I am about to suggest will almost certainly procure you an invitation. But you must weigh up which is of greater importance to you – attending the dance and risking rumours of pushiness attaching to you, or maintaining your dignity while missing out on the fertile opportunities for advancement which such an occasion would offer.*

Ask eight of your friends whom you know to have re-

ceived invitations to the dance to have dinner at your house on the night in question. On securing their acceptances you may then take one of two steps. If you suspect that the hostess rather likes you, and only a lack of pushiness on her part has prevented her from sending you an invitation to her dance, then you may telephone her and enquire whether you might accompany your entire party when it leaves for her dance after dinner.

If, on the other hand, you suspect her attitude towards you may be one of indifference, or even hostility, then you may ask a third party to intervene on your behalf. One of your own friends who is attending the dinner in your house should ring the hostess and, pretending that you are unaware of her request, enquire whether or not you could be invited on the grounds of your joint early evening engagement. It is unlikely that she will refuse.

ADVICE TO A SCHOOLGIRL WISHING TO ATTEND AN OLDER GIRL'S PARTY

Q. I am a pupil at Bryanston. I happen to know that a girl in the year above me is giving a party at her father's house in Hampshire to which I would give anything to be invited. The thing is that, though we have talked twice and she has smiled at me six times, she does not really know me well enough to ask me. The invitations have not gone out yet but I know the party is on Saturday, 16th June. What should I do about it?   A.W., Dorset

A. *Why not arrange to stay over the relevant weekend with a relation or friend who has suitable sporting facilities, such as tennis courts or a swimming pool, and who lives close to the Hampshire house of your idol's father. You may then approach your idol and suggest that she come over on the Sunday and make use of these sporting facilities. This will give her the opportunity to say, 'Oh how lovely (either yes or no). Well, if you are going to be in the area you must come to my party on the Saturday night.'*

Voluntary Work and Charities

One of the rewarding side-effects of doing charity work is that one almost always gets back at least as much as one puts in. Many of our most successful socialisers have found that they have reaped undreamt of dividends in the line of social advancement purely through fortuitous encounters they have made in the line of their charitable duty.

Q. I am moving to London with my husband for three years only. We know everyone in La Paz, where we come from, but we know only ten people in London. I must be very straightforward with you. We are both handsome and we have a lot of money, but I hear it is hard to get quickly into English society. As we have only three years, we wonder if you can tell us of a short-cut to the top?

M. de la C., LaPaz

A. *Your most sensible course will be to offer your services as voluntary workers for one of the leading gay charities. Many of the most social and popular gay men are also best friends with the most social and popular hostesses and you should find that your short-cut to the top is made doubly easy by working for a gay charity than for a 'straight' one.*

A Bachelor Seeks Advice on Maximising his Popularity

Q. I am a twenty-five-year-old bachelor. I am quite good looking, but not particularly. I earn only a moderate salary, but I am rather good company. How can I maximise my social potential?

P.W., N.W.3

A. *Why not put off getting married till you are forty? Bachelors who are not gay, psychopathic or drunk are at a premium over the age of about twenty-nine and any bachelor of even medium quality will find himself to be quite inundated with invitations if he can spin out his single status.*

Climbing in the Art World

Despite the earlier instructions issued about the necessity of shared references and experiences, one exception concerns those who are interested in cultivating friends in the art world. Unfortunately, the major Cork Street galleries who deal in 'Bank Vault' art have now put a stop to the private views they once held at cocktail time. Then, all of informed London could gatecrash, drink excessive quantities of wine at the gallery's expense and interact with a wide mix of people who vaguely shared an interest in the art being shown.

In Thatcher times Cork Street has replaced such freeloading evenings with buyers' lunches, by invitation only, for sober Japanese businessmen and other known buyers. Yet one can still attend openings at less grand galleries such as the Albemarle in Dover Street. The purpose? Purely reconnoitring, though the uninhibited and open-minded nature of many of those others present may well mean that one can meet new and congenial strangers and go out to dinner with them afterwards.

A Note on Accomplices

It is a good idea to have an accomplice who can leak flattering information about you to selected groups on a *quid pro quo* basis which will enhance your image and make your passage smoother.

Problems of Image Linked to Social Rank

Q. Through various measures, including winning a scholarship to Eton, I have made a number of connections which are thought by certain of those who attended primary school with me to be 'poncey'. They also think that I have climbed above my station. I am getting married on the 4th of next month at a church in my own home town and I have been tipped off that certain of those people intend to doorstep the ceremony and make fun of me. What should I do about this?   S.D., Worcs

A. *Why not arrange to have an engagement photograph of yourself and your fiancée printed in the local paper, coupled with a small story about the forthcoming marriage which deliberately gives the time of the ceremony (or even the day) erroneously. None of your* bona fide *guests will pay any attention to the time given in the paper as their invitations will be standing on their mantelpieces giving the correct time. This should successfully serve to eliminate unwelcome guests at the ceremony.*

THE POSH GROCER PROBLEM

Q. I am not a malicious person but I feel a certain local grocer in my neighbourhood needs a bit of corrective training. This shop, let us call it Monkbacks, has been catering for the more sophisticated palates of the many very rich and titled people in our area for a hundred years and it seems that with each passing year the grocers themselves feel they have become grander. My family and I always have a laugh at their extremely refined voices when we go in there. My family, although untitled, has owned our house in the village for five hundred years. I was therefore slightly upset when Mrs Monkback exhibited indecent haste in despatching me, mid-order, when she spied a certain local earl approaching the counter. How can I take this ludicrous family down a peg or two?   V.E., Berks

A. *Many local papers regularly print letters from colonial correspondents who, having learned that their ancestors lived in that area, require information about any extant relatives, however distant, that they might have. The letters often go on to give colourful details of the family history preceding its emigration to the colonies.*

   The grocer you mention has a rather distinctive name and I feel it would be amusing for you to arrange for a friend in the colonies to post for you a letter written roughly along the following lines:

> *My name is Monkback and I am trying to trace my family history. All I know is that my ancestors were rat-catchers and hereditary night-soil collectors around 1870 and that my forebear, Harold Monkback, was the last convict to be sent to Australia for the quaint crime of impersonating a gentleman. Please would anyone who can give me any further information write to me at this address.*

You may then, by pre-arrangement with your colonial friend, give an address to which correspondence should be sent.

There is no reason why your local paper would not oblige the author of this letter by printing it and you might even rub salt in the wound, on your next visit to the shop, by thoughtfully presenting Mrs Monkback with a cutting 'in case you had missed it. Extremely interesting, No?'

SUCKING UP TO OLD PEOPLE

Q. What advice would you give to someone, eager to advance socially, who has come to London with no money, no friends, a bedsit in the suburbs, but four invitations to rather smart parties, procured in a rather illicit manner?

A.W., Greenwich

A. *The top tip for social infiltrators is that, on entering any room where a party is being held, they should immediately make a beeline for the oldest person in the room.*

Not only is such a person likely to be the most interesting person in the room, he or she is also likely to be an owner of a large and centrally positioned flat or house, which may well have room for a charming young person recently arrived in London with no friends.

Old people love young people and like to have them in close proximity. Hosts and hostesses will be very glad to see someone talking to their great aunt, or whoever she might be, and they will ask you again.

Naturally, you would not proceed were you to feel an antipathy towards the old person, but presuming that you find their company enjoyable you will see that there are bounteous advantages to such a friendship.

Like a pilot fish you can 'latch on' to the multiple friend-ships which will have been forged over the many years of socialising that the old person has undertaken. You may also enjoy the comfortable entertainment facilities of a central residence, whether or not you are actually living in it.

Showing other People that you are Titled

Q. I have recently become titled. How should I best let this be generally known?   Anon

A. *Many newly titled people who feel an urgent need that their new position should be fully comprehended by inter-locutors use the method of telling long and seemingly point-less anecdotes about incidents involving themselves. The raison d'être of such stories is, of course, that at some point the narrator will be addressed by his or her title.*

A much less blatant method is the widely used cheque-writing strategy. Many shopkeepers report that titled people are conspicuous by their eagerness to write cheques for insignificant sums, despite obviously bulging pockets filled with wads of notes.

A third method used by one newly appointed countess is to carry a needlepoint cushion cover whose pattern is de-signed to bear the surname of her son and his arms. This enables her to lay down the needlepoint with a sigh of exhaustion after a couple of minutes of stitching and exclaim loudly, 'Oh you know I can't get this finished. By the time its done, his grandfather will be dead and he'll be Sherwood.'

Dealing with the Nouveau Riche

Q. I live in Norfolk and it is a matter of intense annoyance to me that the wife of a local industrialist has moved into the area and has blocked off a track to the freshes which has been used by every local since time immemorial to get to the beach where many boats are moored. The track does not even go past the house of the woman in question. In fact, her own house is on a hill about half a mile away and she clearly uses the house as an observation point from which she watches with a telescope before racing down in her Range Rover to berate people for trespassing. How can I punish her?   J.G.H., Binham

A. *Why not telephone her, posing as a representative of the BBC, asking if she would be willing to take part in a pro-gramme being made about the real-life counterparts of soap* opera characters. *Explain that enquiries made locally have elicited a wide response that she is extremely like the character of Lynda in the Archers (a character whose failings are extremely similar to those of the woman you mention).*

SOCIALIST SOCIALISER

Q. I wish to be prepared for the social effects of a possible Labour victory at the next election. Can you give me the names of some key left-wing social figures I could be cultivating as a precautionary measure.   F.W., W.2

A. *Paul Foot, Lord Kennet, John Lloyd, Martin Jacques, many Bonham Carters, Peter Melchett and John Smith.*

KISSING NOISES

Q. What is the correct sound to emit when kissing a friend by way of greeting or farewell?

C.D., Greenwich, near London

A. *It seems that 'Mwa!' has recently been superceded by 'Mwu!'. 'Mmm!' is currently not acceptable.*

BUSINESS CARDS

Q. I recently met an attractive young woman while attending the opening of the new Berkeley Square gallery in Bruton Street. She laughed mockingly when I asked her if she had a business card (I know she is in business) so I wondered if it is not done to carry a business card any more?   M.D.

A. *Business cards are considered very undesirable these days and at every instance it is preferable to write your name and number in handwriting on a piece of paper.*

Despatching unwelcome callers who have dropped in without ringing first.

LONDON LIFE

MANY UNLANDED SOPHISTICATES FIND themselves living in London for part or all of that key social decade which takes one from roughly twenty to roughly thirty.

Before twenty, people are at school, university or travelling. After thirty, people are less interested in showing off their figures, clothes and friends under epilepsy-inducing conditions such as strobe lights or riots. They are more drawn to pursuits such as eating and lolling back on sofas in spacious country houses with real fires crackling in the grate, and they begin to drift away from London.

As the main reason for living in London is to round up enough friends with whom to spend time in the country, people generally find that a decade of rounding them up is quite sufficient to ensure a stockpile of stimulators who can be invited up, down or over to one's country house, once one has moved there. Some stimulators are even likely to have moved nearby, into separate yet adjacent rural accommodation of their own.

Other sophisticates stay more than a decade in London – for reasons linked to careers or ownership of attractive and centrally located London property. Yet overtures of friendship made by all but the most outstandingly attractive new arrivals in the capital towards these older sophisticates will fall on stony ground, as red-headed American Michael Vermeulen found when he first hit London.

'Know how many English homes I've been into in the six months I've been here?', the intelligent and successful Vermeulen was wont to accuse colleagues on the glossy magazine where he worked, 'Two.'

'Know what was actually said to me by an English person and she genuinely meant it? "Most English people find they already have too many friends"'. His audience would nod in silent agreement.

Unfortunately, it is true. Londoners over thirty have already made their group of friends and have subconsciously closed their list – mainly out of mental laziness.

For this reason it is important to arrive in London early in one's twenties to allow oneself a greater scope of potential circles to break into. The most desirable circles will close their membership soonest, simply because of stimulation overload.

This brings to mind a conversation which took place between a key hostess and Lesley Cunliffe, writer and idolisee of many of her acquaintances. Lesley was then thirty-one and already had a surfeit of friends on her 'books'.

Hostess: 'You must meet Giles Wordsworth, he's the most riveting figure. Brilliantly clever, hilariously funny, fascinating life story . . .'

'No!' whispered Lesley, from her day bed, where she was recovering from 'no ordinary hangover, this must be some kind of a mini-stroke' – 'No, please don't introduce him. I couldn't stand any more stimuli'.

Rejection or acceptance – neither will be possible if one cannot even find accommodation in London in the first place.

FINDING ACCOMMODATION IN LONDON

A major contributing cause towards Glasgow's becoming the cultural capital of Britain is that exciting new young people from the provinces are not barred from finding accommodation there as they are in London where renting is only practical if deductible as a business expense.

There is no possibility today of seeing an advert in the *Evening Standard* with an apartment going for rent at a reasonable price. Even if such an advertisement were ever inserted, the property in question would have been snapped up by the person in advertising sales who took the details before it came anywhere near being printed.

Why, even Harold Evans used to go up to the publishing stone of an evening, when he was editing *The Times*, to look for suitable accommodation for himself.

Aside from having access to a London property owned by one's family, or having enough money to take out a mortgage oneself, there are only two ways in which a young person on normal income can come to the capital and live with a degree of dignity. One, as a lodger paying peppercorn rent to a friend who owns property. Two, by performing part-time duties as nanny, au-pair, butler or companion (live-in) to someone whose own accommodation is reasonable.

Failing either of these, you may as well go back to wherever you came from in the provinces, or alternatively try Glasgow.

LIVING IN TOOTING

Q. I have been offered a room to rent in quite a nice house in Tooting. It is only sixty pounds a week. Do you think I should take it? A.McN.W., Alton, Hants

A. *No. It will take exactly the same amount of time to commute from Hampshire by British Rail as from Tooting into an area of London where you can find social diversion. Quite apart from this, the real cost of the room will be £120 per week as you will undoubtedly spend another £60 on taxis. Why not save yourself two and a half hours of travelling time per day, and simply pay £120 a week to rent a room in Chelsea at the outset?*

SOMEWHERE TO PARK

Q. I have a flat in Fulham but my mother's house is in Chelsea. Can I therefore get resident's parking for Kensington and Chelsea by giving the Chelsea address to the DVLC for my vehicle registration document? D.McC.

A. *It would be inadvisable to do so. A recent witch hunt in the Kensington and Chelsea parking control office has exposed a number of culprits practising this very method of deception. Permits have been stripped from car windscreens by plain-clothes officials who had looked up suspects on the electoral roll and found their residential address to be different from that of their Vehicle Registration Document. Snoopers even waited outside the houses of suspects in order to determine residence. The maximum penalty is £2000 and the likelihood of arrest so great that many MPs I have spoken to recently have decided to go without a Kensington and Chelsea permit rather than run the risk of public exposure.*

PROTOCOL PECULIAR TO LONDON

Q. What is the correct protocol concerning dropping in

without ringing first?   J.H.

A. *It entirely depends on whether you are in London or in the country. The stress involved in living in London and the very surfeit of people one comes across in day-to-day life means that the home must be respected as a refuge which should not be penetrated without prior warning. Even teenagers should not drop in on one another in London. In remoter areas of the country dropping in is an accepted tradition, but London rules apply to neo- and juxta-London households.*

Avoiding Droppers-in

Q. I have just moved into a fashionable square in the middle of the King's Road, having come down from Oxford in the summer and not yet found a job. I am at home a lot during the day. As a result the doorbell goes about five times a day with people dropping in without ringing first, simply because they were 'passing'. I don't always want to see them, not because I am particularly busy but because I am not. How can I deal with this problem?   D.McN., S.W.3

A. *Make it a policy always to put on your coat and hat before answering the door. In this way you can say, 'Hi! I was just going out', if the caller is unwelcome.*

Dangers of Assault

Q. My seventeen-year-old daughter has lived a protected life of blissful ignorance – so far. She simply does not believe that it is dangerous to travel on public transport or to walk home alone late at night. Though we usually give her enough money to ensure she takes a taxi back from some of the dreadful dumps she likes to go for a night out from school, she often spends this on extra drinks or make-up and then has to be driven home by a drunkard or travel on the Tube, risking Clockwork Orange-style assaults. What can we do about it?   A.St C., Campden Hill, W.8

A. *Instead of giving her the taxi money before she leaves for the evening, it should be deposited in a jam-jar, lightly disguised by leaves in your front garden. In this way she can always afford a taxi home, even if she has spent all the money she has on her.*

POLL TAX PROBLEMS

Q. I am an actor. Four years ago I moved to a house in the country where I have a mortgage and am registered for tax purposes, etc. When in London I stay in a friend's flat at the above address and as this has worked well I registered for a double vote and also for a permit to park the car in this area. I now find that I will be expected to pay two lots of poll tax. I approached an official at Kensington and Chelsea who was sympathetic and instantly deleted me by putting a line through my form. He was about to clear me off the computer until I pointed out that it didn't solve my parking problem. Is there any way around this situation, or am I going to have to have a very expensive car permit?

J.F.B., Holland Park, W.11

A. *The solution is to transfer the documents pertaining to your car and its ownership into the name of a trusted friend who lives in the Royal Borough and would be willing to pass on the various documents from DVLC and RBKC to you as they fall through his letterbox. Have yourself listed as a named driver. You will have to forego the double vote.*

TIPS FOR HARMONIOUS LONDON LIVING

One of the hidden expenses of living in London is the cost of restaurants. A common mistake made by people already paying exorbitant rentals or mortgages is to try to budget by failing to engage a daily. This will prove a false economy to those living in households made up of more than two people.

Imagine the scenario of three young flat-sharers returning from work at the typical London time of seven p.m. (Even Bond Street to Sydney Street takes twenty tension-rich minutes by taxi.) Quite apart from the fact that each one of them will think the other two should 'clear up' the inevitable debris of the kitchen, all three of them will be genuinely too physically tired to do it.

Inexorably they will be drawn to a restaurant – at its

cheapest, a Pizza Express. Therefore they will spend between them £36 when they could have spent £16: £6 on a daily to wash up, £10 on quality food and drink. This means that between them they are wasting £140 pounds a week through not having a daily.

TRICKING FLAT MATE INTO PAYING TOWARDS A DAILY

Q. I have a great deal of trouble with a friend who shares my rented accommodation. He is charming but his standards of personal hygiene are far below the average. Like a snail, he leaves in his wake the evidence of where he has been – cigarette butts in coffee cups, crumpled £10 notes on the ground, a trail of newspapers, etc. He cannot believe, however, that he is untidy, and therefore refuses to contribute to a daily. What should I do?   M.W., S.W.3

A. *As you say this person is very absent-minded, why not nip into his bedroom and take, say, £25 from his trouser pocket at the start of each week. This way you can buy up to six hours of dailying at the current rate of £4.50-£5.00 per hour without either of you feeling any resentment.*

CONVERSATION
(AND FLATTERY)

CONVERSATION IS PROBABLY THE pre-eminent skill to be mastered by seekers after social success. Some may argue that the skills of flirtation and seduction will give greater social potency, but they are forgetting a key factor. While certain roués and rouées do indeed enjoy a marked popularity amongst members of the opposite sex to their own, the very nature of that popularity will serve to arouse jealousy in members of their own sex and so will alienate them from roughly 37% of all potential social recruits.

What is wonderful about the skill of conversation is that it takes in listening as well as talking. Even if, therefore, one finds quite early on in one's career as a socialiser that one's prowess at monoloquy is limited, that one's observations are un-original, that one's memory for gossip is frustratingly in-efficient, it need not matter. 'There are people who instead of listening to what is being said to them are already listening to what they are going to say themselves,' said Albert Guinon; and as such people make up a surprising proportion of the popu-lace, the inadequate talker need only work on acquiring the much simpler skill of listening. This is the central tenet of the world's great finishing schools who send forth acceptable socialisers each year culled from the most unpromising material.

TALK, DON'T TALK

Q. I am feeling a bit paranoid because I went to the loo during dinner at a friend's house the other night, and as I was coming back down the stairs to the dining room I stopped by a mirror on the landing to admire myself. As I was quietly pulling various faces in the mirror, I overheard the follow-ing conversation about myself.

'It's really sweet that you're still so devoted to Clarissa', someone was saying to a former boyfriend of mine who was sitting at the table. 'What is it about her that's caused you to carry a candle all these years?'

My former boyfriend replied, 'Well, we live in a very un-certain world, everything's changing every day, no one stays in the same place for very long, marriages break up, relationships break up, but there's one thing that I can always depend on as being constant. Wherever I am in the world, and wherever Clarissa is, I can know for certain that she will be thinking or talking about herself.'

The table broke into roars of laughter and it was obvious that everyone there thought I talked about myself a lot of the time. So I went down, and I said . . . (Requirements of space necessitated the editing of this letter but it ended with the request that the correspondent, having been thus chagrined, now wished to be advised on the general principles of successful listening to the conversations of others when she was, frankly, quite egotistical and not actually interested in what anyone else might have to say unless it concerned herself. Yet she was nervous about failing social popularity.)
C.P., W.12

NODDING

At one stage in the recent past people who wished to pretend to be listening to what others were saying would nod a lot to suggest that they were taking in fresh points as the talk proceeded. This technique has, however, now been discredited. Too many television film editors have failed to edit out the back views of continuously nodding heads during interviews and, now, nodding immediately excites the suspicion (a) that you are not listening or (b) that you are being patronising.

Nodding should now be substituted by a gamut of facial gestures, such as raising the eyebrows at appropriate moments, snorting, sighing and furrowing the brows. Needless to say, the eyes must not be seen to wander further from the speaker's face than to one's glass or plate.

Every so often it may be necessary to put new questions to the person to whom one is 'listening' purely out of politeness, as the talker will soon become uncomfortable if he or she feels they are broaching fresh topics unbidden.

Useful catch queries include: 'But what did you really think about him/her?'; 'What do you really think should be done, then?'; and 'So what did you end up thinking?' These are useful for moments when one has not listened to a word and is in danger of being rumbled.

TIPS FOR CONVERSATIONALISTS FROM THE LOWER INTELLIGENCE BRACKET

Q. Since I left school last summer (I went to Cranbourne Chase), I have been invited to lots and lots of parties and things but I really don't know what to say to people. Do you think it would be a good idea for me to start smoking dope? That way I wouldn't really have to say much – just smile knowingly. At school they called me 'Lights' for 'The lights are on but no one is at home,' but I am really pretty.

C.A., Chippenham

A. *Many of London's most sought-after party-goers say little or nothing while out on the circuit, but dope-smoking is really very passé now and not at all suitable for the more thrusting and achieving ethos of today, although many school leavers do use the device as an effective way of disguising intellectual inadequacy. Concentrate instead on cultivating a mysterious image. Invest in having flowers sent to yourself – the enclosed card should simply read 'R', a good all-purpose initial. Be seen with a curious and unpredictable range of literature:* Code Breaking in the Second World War *or* The Song of Maldoror, *for example. Change the subject when people question your choice. Go into the Underground and pick up some discarded tickets from baffling locations such as Theydon Bois. Leave these around for people to see. At all costs avoid saying anything. You may coast through for years.*

GOSSIP

The practice of gossiping is much maligned. After all, if gossip is true, what harm in disseminating it? Though of course one should tread carefully where the stability of happy regimes can be undermined by rumours of instability in its higher echelons.

Normal gossip, however, where one person might reveal to another the secret defects of a third party, is more likely to be instructive than destructive. Why should a man have to wait, for example, until the memoirs of a former heart-throb are published posthumously to find that the real reason for her rejection of his suit was that she had developed a bizarre but exclusive romantic predilection for Chinese traffic wardens only?

Equally, when a friend is making you feel inadequate about certain aspects of, for example, your marriage, which you had not previously noted were undesirable, would it not be constructive of a third party with factual information to step forward to inform you that your friend was only 'projecting' the problems of her own marriage on to your own?

So much of gossip in high society centres around the basic need to discover defects in those glamorous people who, by their very apparent perfection, serve to make others feel inadequate.

But gossip is not comprised solely of negative material. One also wants to know about advances in careers, the names of surprising cousins of mutual acquaintances, the sort of breakfasts favoured by certain eccentric earls, that sort of thing.

Anything which offers one an insight into the motivations of other people can help one progress to an understanding of life in leaps and bounds and it will do the pious more harm than good to close his or her ears to such instructive information.

And in any case, we often discuss other people 'behind their backs' purely so that the company present can have a good opinion of our judgement rather than for any love or disparagement we might feel to the person we mention.

ENCOURAGING INDISCRETION

Q. I have a friend who only says good things about other people. I know for a fact that she is privy to lots of exciting information as she works in a certain West End gallery where there are always dramas being played out by glamorous and interesting people, but she has obviously taken the view 'if you can't say something good about someone, don't say anything at all'. How can I encourage her to pep up her conversation as I fear her invitations will soon begin to dry up?   B.L., Maida Vale

A. *Why not encourage her by insisting that she is a 'brilliant mimic'?*

'You don't realise,' you can assert, 'how you can bring a

person to life, just by mentioning their name. It's obviously unconscious, if you're unaware of it. But even if somebody else just mentions the name of someone you know, you immediately start to take on their bearing, their facial expressions, it's absolutely brilliant.

'Do please mimic so and so? Oh, do please, just even say one typical sentence.' With group encouragement you should soon see results as she unwittingly starts to give away gratifying indiscretions.

TRICKING PEOPLE INTO ADMITTING THEY ARE HAVING AN AFFAIR

Q. I strongly suspect that one of my closest friends is having an affair with someone I used to fancy, but she will not admit it, partly because she loves being secretive and, partly, I think, because she thinks I still fancy him, which I don't. How can I trick them into a confession?   M.G.C., Paris

A. *The following method may prove successful in releasing the information to satisfy your curiosity, but, as you will see, the timing will be crucial.*

Wait for an evening when you know your close friend to be out of town. Then ring the answerphone of her suspected suitor and, holding your nose, leave the following message.

'Darling, it's me. I've got such a bad cold I can hardly speak. Please ring me on. . . .' Then give the number of another friend of your own, who is willing to serve as accomplice, and who is not known to either of the two suspected romantic partners.

With any luck your former 'fancy' will ring the answerphone of your accomplice and leave an incriminating message. Later he will presume that his answerphone message must have come from a misrouted caller. After all, all she said was 'darling'.

OTHER MEANS OF TRICKING PEOPLE INTO TELLING YOU OTHER THINGS

Many people will eagerly go halfway towards meeting someone who is trying to cajole information out of them which they feel guilty about releasing. The main device used by experienced gossips to secure data is to pretend that they 'already know' what they suspect, and wish to have confirmed.

Q. I strongly suspect that someone in my office named Sarah has found another job and is planning to leave quite soon. It would be convenient for me to be able to confirm that this is the case, as it would mean that I could then arrange for another friend of mine to stand by to apply for her post. Sarah and I have a friend in common but, though I have hinted at my suspicions, and she has smirked knowingly, she has obviously been sworn to secrecy. How can I get her to tell me the facts? G.D., Hinden

A. *First engage Sarah in general conversation about, for example, where she might be going for her forthcoming holiday. Then ring up the mutual friend and casually slip into your conversation the following remark: 'By the way, Sarah's told me her news'. If this then leads to a confirmation of your suspicion, you can then say, 'Oh goodness. How interesting. That wasn't the news I was talking about actually. I was talking about the fact that she's been invited to Barbados on holiday. That's very exciting too, isn't it?'*

FLATTERY

What really flatters a man is that you think him worth flattering.

George Bernard Shaw

Even confident and amusing talkers, whose repertoires are replete with anecdotes, profundities and new gossip, can find that listening is a skill which will ultimately pay them more dividends in the self-popularising stakes than will talking.

Flattery, however, is a yet more efficient means of self-advancement than listening and does not even require any special skills of subtlety.

Flattery is music to the ears of even the most highly intelligent and suspicious agent of MI5 and it is a reflection on human gullibility and vanity that flattery should be the secret weapon of many of our most successful heart-breakers.

That is not to say that flattery need ever be insincere. Why, one can easily stick to praising things about another person that are genuinely praiseworthy. In certain cases, however, these may be difficult to locate.

PRAISING PEOPLE LESS ADEQUATE THAN ONESELF

Q. As I become more and more powerful and rich (I know I can write frankly) I find myself becoming rather compulsively patronising to others – particularly to younger males. In my social life I do find myself quite frequently faced with admiring young men (most of them looking for jobs in banking) and I suffer from retrospective embarrassment when I think of the fulsome flattery that has issued from my lips as I try to overcompensate.   Name and address withheld.

A. *In these situations it is probably better to limit your verbal output. Simply nod sagely and cast the occasional faintly complicit glance at your interlocutor. This will ultimately be far more flattering than damning him with faint praise.*

FLATTERING A HOSTESS FOLLOWING A SUCCESSFUL DINNER

Q. How much should one flatter someone who has given one an especially good dinner when telephoning or writing to thank them?   L.G., Andover

A. *It should be sufficient to mention only two specific things. For example, having commented on the quality of the food and how much you enjoyed meeting certain fellow guests, it would be fulsome to mention how attractive your host or hostess him- or herself was looking as well. As a rule of thumb, most people would prefer commentary on how attractive they themselves had looked to commentary on the quality of the food served.*

FLATTERING PEOPLE AS A MEANS OF GETTING THEM TO GO OUT WITH YOU

Despite the regularly publicised reports of psychologists that people tend to mate with others who are of the same general degree of attractiveness as themselves, one often sees exceptions to this rule. There are many notable examples of marriages between slim, young and exquisite girls and fat, old and rather dull men, who may not even be particularly rich. Equally one often sees the example of startlingly attractive men married to startlingly unattractive women.

Successful flattery is the secret behind such relationships and one need only count how many of them are solemnised between glamorous members of the acting profession to unglamorous partners to realise that this is the case. To an actor, flattery is the very breath of life and the marital partners of such people often qualify for their role by being willing to provide a dependable and continuous service of praise and reassurance.

ATTRACTING A BEAUTIFUL WOMAN THROUGH FLATTERY WHEN ONE IS HIDEOUS ONESELF

Q. I am a forty-five-year-old don at Oxford. I have to say that I am not the world's best-looking man but I have fallen in love with someone who, though rather spoilt and silly, is probably the most beautiful woman I have ever seen. How should I best go about making my bid for her affections? I do write rather good poetry. Should I compose an ode to her beauty, or do you think my own looks would count against me to too great an extent for it to be worth my while trying?

T.L., Oxford

A. *On the contrary, you are, as an intellectual, in a stronger position than many other men. Beautiful women are not particularly pleased to be told they are beautiful. After all, they did nothing to deserve it, so it is not much of a compliment. On the other hand, many beauties, faute de another complex, worry that they are not thought to be intelligent. Why not flatter her, therefore, about her intelligence?*

This method proved efficacious in a previous correspondent who deluged his prey with copies of the works of Proust and George Steiner on the grounds that she was 'one of the few people I know who will really appreciate this'.

It should not be long before your targeted partner begins to associate you in her mind with pleasure, the pleasure of her own ego having been boosted. This pleasure may soon translate itself into romantic ardour.

How can I prevent my son from having an affair with one of my best friends? He is

eighteen, she is forty-six, and the whole thing is appalling.

ROMANCE

THE MODERN PASSAGE TOWARDS finding a suitable life-long partner is invariably booby-trapped with potential for humiliation, depression and guilt. It can be particularly hazardous for victims of the philosophy spawned in the Beatles era (see footnote 1).

Yet romance-seekers who have emerged from this passage, having finally found satisfaction, will invariably look back with laughter and even retrospective gratitude at the pitfalls that once punctured their *amour propre*.

Even if the most fervently convinced pubescents could wave a wand and secure the romantic partner that they genuinely know they will always love, they would be disconcerted were their wish to be granted. That Concordesque route of immediate gratification would be ultimately much less rewarding to them. It would be less interesting and less educational, for comparative purposes, than the 'overland' route with its multiple overnight stops and false trails which most of us are forced to take before arriving at our goal.

There are, however, key danger zones to be avoided along the way – zones where damage can be inflicted on more than just the ego.

RAKES AND ROUÉS

Rakes and roués have proliferated in the last thirty years and we have even witnessed the phenomenon of rakesses and roueés since *Cosmopolitan* magazine was first published in this country. Such figures are the Jabberwockies of romanticland, yet encounters with them are inevitable.

---

1. Some comments made recently by the seventy-seven-year-old gardener at the Yorkshire headquarters of social leader Jo Farrell struck me as having peculiar profundity. Fred Wilkinson had been reading the front page of the *Daily Mirror*. He suddenly looked up and said, 'You know when everything started to go wrong with the world? It was when them Beatles came along with their long hair and their Yeah Yeah Yeahs'.

Yes, romance was more romantic before them Beatles came along, but given that they've been along, we must examine means of dealing with the havoc left in their wake.

RAKE'S PROGRESS

Q. I recently had a whirlwind romance with a man I met through my interest in rowing. He has been involved with the sport for some years, and though he is not my type, he bowled me over with the intensity of his emotion. I cannot understand why I have not heard from him since the night we met when he seemed to be passionately keen on me. Should I telephone him, or do you think I could have done something wrong? M.T., S.W.15

A. *I have had a number of enquiries which mention the same man so I am afraid it is likely that his intentions were in-sincere. There are many men like this on the social circuit and in my view their names should be blacklisted as are those of credit-card abusers.*

ROAD TO ROUÉ

Q. My rather young girlfriend of twenty has been seduced away from me by someone of thirty-seven whom I know to be a complete creep, womaniser and layabout. She is spend-ing almost every evening sleeping with him at his flat. He is horribly cunning about covering his tracks and she has no idea she is only one of about three women he is 'running'. How can I get her back, or at least get her away from him? O.M., W.12

A. *Pretend to have lost interest in her yourself. Meanwhile bombard her boyfriend's flat with implicative postcards in varying hands. Like all women she will take a keen interest in the postal deliveries received by her suitor, and it should not be long before a severance in the liaison is naturally brought about.*

MARRIAGE BEFORE REACHING FULL ADULTHOOD

The legal age of adulthood was twenty-one until 1970 when the Labour government reduced it to eighteen so that juvenile idealists could vote for their Party at the next election. It was a cruel act because it has meant that people who are unsuitably matched, yet whose judgement is distorted by surges of hor-monal activity, can legally commit themselves to one another in marriage without their parents' consent.

Now parents can do little other than grimly attend the ceremonies as grotesque mismatches between juveniles are solemnised on a daily basis. They can only hope that no progeny will result before the decrees nisi come through.

The next Labour government might do well to consider raising the legal age of adulthood to twenty-three as increased life expectancy has 'put back' most stages of human development and many youths of today spin out their childhood until their twenty-sixth birthday.

STOPPING ONE'S DAUGHTER FROM MARRYING UNSUITABLY

Q. How can I prevent my lovely seventeen-year-old daughter from marrying someone who is entirely unworthy of her? My husband and I moved to Wales in the early 1970s to bring up our children in idyllic rural surroundings. What we entirely overlooked was that, on the surfacing of adolescent passion, it would be focused, *faute de mieux,* on one of the only two local youths of her age-group. He is bald, squat and generally unattractive, and the passage of time will show them to be incompatible. So far we have carefully disguised our disapproval. What should we do to prevent them from becoming engaged?   M.P., Crickhowell

A. *No greater disincentive towards teenage marriage than parental approval exists. Therefore you should continue to conceal your true feelings. On the contrary, you should appear to be so approving that you commission a set of expensive portraits of the couple together. Have massive blow-ups made of the least flattering frame numbers and position these around the house. Meanwhile, invite some of your old friends from London, with attractive teenage children, to come down and stay for a bit.*

STOPPING ONE'S SON FROM GOING OUT WITH ONE'S BEST FRIEND

Q. My son is doing A-levels at Westminster and we have allowed him to move into our basement. To our horror he has begun an affair with someone whom I previously considered to be one of my best friends, and it is taking place right under our noses, so to speak. We have pretended so far not to realise what is happening but are desperate to

71

stop it. The whole thing is appalling. He is eighteen and she
is forty-two. A.C., W.8

A. *You should pretend to be delighted by the match and encourage the couple to spend a lot of time together. Invite the
friend to move into the basement and start to throw a series
of lunch or dinner parties made up of schoolboys and meno-
pausal women. The age disparity, thus highlighted in Monty
Python manner, should soon begin to disconcert the couple
and an early termination to the liaison can be expected.*

PARTICULAR PROBLEMS OF SOPHISTICATES

The multiple choices available to sophisticates and people who
are overtly good-looking can work to their long-term disadvantage. Confused by having no limit on their parameters of
potential behaviour, they can become serial daters as they
search for increasingly stimulating 'kicks' to be provided by
their partners.

Soon they must search for younger and younger partners as
they exhaust those available in their own age bracket. The
early warning signals of their reputation and their facial expressions, often frozen in time to recapture a successful seduction, or set in a mask of studied flirtatiousness, still do nothing
to prevent successive generations falling briefly under their
spell.

A DAUGHTER IN DANGER

Q. I am terribly worried about my daughter. She is lovely looking, and virtually every man she meets is most obviously
attracted to her. Already, at sixteen, she is beginning to
become terribly blasé, rather like one of those ghastly
characers in a Bret Easton Ellis book. The only difference is
that our family is stable and united.

What on earth can I do to dent her self-confidence for an
instructive period of time? She is really becoming far too
arrogant for her own good? R.H., Long Island

A. *No female, no matter how flawless a figure she might have, is
invulnerable to anxieties that she is somehow defective, and
usually that she is overweight. Why not pop down to a
glazier in your area who provides distorted glass for fair-*

ground mirrors and order a full-length 'primary enlarging' strip which gives only minimal distortion. Have it framed attractively and hung in your own home, preferably in your daughter's bathroom. It is unlikely that she will develop anorexia if all other areas of her life are progressing satisfactorily, but a few months of seeing herself as physically flawed will do no harm and may encourage her to work on other areas of her personality.

HELPING FRIENDS WITH THEIR ROMANTIC LIVES

Many of us stand by in impotent horror as our friends become involved in romantic liaisons which, it is immediately clear to an independent observer, have no hope of succeeding. Other friends seem to fail to become involved in any romantic liaison whatsoever, despite their being extremely attractive, rich and interesting.

While men who enjoy the aforementioned qualities are swiftly snapped up as soon as they come on the market, these same men tend to be passive about pass-making. Therefore they have to be 'got', albeit subtly, by women. This means that those women who do not engage in research and careful strategic planning can be left suitorless, or even have their existing suitor taken away from them.

Before going on to examine possible strategies let us not overlook the much-underrated cause of romantic inefficiency – astrology.

HELPING A FRIEND WHO ALLOWS ASTROLOGY TO BLIGHT HER POTENTIAL HAPPINESS

Q. My best friend is causing me a lot of angst because I can see quite clearly the path she should take towards happiness, but for reasons of primitive superstition she is refusing to take it.

What has happened is that she was going out with someone who had been in love with her for years, and everything was going swimmingly. She, too, was in love with him. However, she always reads her horoscope, particularly those by Patrick Walker, whom she insists is absolutely accurate, and she has interpreted his current advice to Geminians as instruction that she should leave this particular man.

What can I do to get them back together?   A.D., N.W.1

A. *As she is superstitious there should be no reason why she should not be approached in the street near her house by a student actress, hired from the Webber Douglas School, in disguise as a gypsy.*

The 'gypsy' should be instructed to buttonhole your friend with some lavender and then offer to read her hand. At this stage she can claim to 'see' quite clearly that your friend has made a grave mistake in rejecting a recent romantic partner, to whom destiny has decreed she should be linked. She may even give the initials of the man in question, depending on the guillibility level of your friend.

It should be only a matter of time before there is a rapprochement.

THEATRICAL MEASURES TO SECURE PARTNERS

Q. I have fallen madly in love with a certain actor. He is not particularly well known but I watched him on a chat show and really feel we are made for each other – and he is a bachelor. I am an actress myself but the chances of our being cast in the same production are terribly remote. How can I stage a meeting with him?   Z.R., S.W.6

A. *All actors are terribly susceptible to flattery and, as you are an actress yourself, you should have no difficulty in putting your skills to the test in the manner which I am about to suggest.*

Approach a close friend and fellow actor to assist you. Posing as a doctor, he or she should contact the agent of the man in question, requesting a bedside visit to a patient who is being nursed at home. 'It's a last-ditch attempt really, that the sound of his voice might help to bring her out of a coma. We know that he is her favourite actor.' The cost of props should be minimal – a couple of white coats, a drip feed, a doctor's bag. Your own home and bedroom can provide the setting.

Provided you are of a reasonably attractive physical appearance it is extremely likely that the actor will develop romantic feelings towards you during the hours he spends at the bedside. Not only will he have a captive audience, your comatose face will be a continual reminder to him of how marvellous he is and he should soon begin to confuse love of himself with love of you.

When you finally 'come to' it should be only a matter of time before you start dating. Were the truth ever to come to light, he would no doubt admire the acting skills that had enabled you to keep your eyes shut over a period of two, three, even four days – however long it is necessary to ensure his attachment.

RIVALS IN LOVE

Having secured your partner, it is important to remember that you must always be on your guard against interlopers. The cliché of men marrying their secretaries or other workmates is an obvious danger.

MAKING ONE'S HUSBAND REPELLENT TO OTHER WOMEN

Q. When my husband first entered Parliament in 1983 I was delighted to see him engage a secretary of considerable bulk, as I know he does not find such women attractive. Now, however, I learn that he has been 'allocated' the services of a very *soignée* research assistant who has just left Oxford and with whom he is to spend every Friday, over a period of six weeks, working on the preparation of a certain paper. How can I prevent them from having an affair?

Name and address supplied.

A. *Refuse all dinner invitations for the Thursday nights preceding the six Fridays of the researcher's term of office. Instead cook at home for your husband, preparing dishes so heavily loaded with garlic that he will be physically repugnant to anyone who comes into proximity. People never know with garlic whether it is garlic or whether it is something to do with the personal hygiene of the offender.*

SHARP PRACTICES

Q. My so-called best friend and I are in pursuit of the same girl. He, however, has the advantage of knowing her phone number. On his birthday he is throwing a dinner for twenty at his flat in Chelsea and has invited her but not me. He has also played dirty by telling her that he has no idea why I dislike her so much. How can I gatecrash the party in a way which will show me in a dignified light?   B.B., Kensington

A. *In the circumstances it would be perfectly fair for you to attend as a singing telegram. You could even make reference in your lyrics to your best friend's duplicity.*

PORK OR BEEF

Q. I recently met a rather attractive television personality named Rowland Rivron at a drinks party. He asked if we could go and 'beef' together. I took offence as I thought this was far too precipitative and so I walked off. Did I do right? I do fancy him and would like to see him again. B.S., E.11

A. *You have made the mistake of confusing 'beef' with 'pork'. Why not telephone Rivron and try to set up a secondary engagement?*

DETERMINING WHETHER OR NOT SOMEONE FANCIES ONE

Q. How can one tell for sure whether or not someone fancies one? I often get the feeling that a certain girl in my office is sending out signals of encouragement. We have had drinks together after work and have enjoyed stimulating and amusing conversation, but I have so far stopped short of making a physical overture. Frankly I would almost prefer not to go out with anyone at all than run the risk of rejection, which would, in this case, be doubly humiliating due to our professional propinquity. Can you suggest anything?   M.McC., S.W.3

A. *Yes. I suggest you take your colleague for drinks at a quiet bar where bench-style seating is available. Sit adjacent to her, then draw the conversation gradually to the topic of adolescent crushes. Laughingly bring up the moment when, as an adolescent, you had a pass made at you by a certain girl whom you thought you had fancied until you had been put off by her unusual kissing technique. 'Shall I demonstrate?' you can chuckle unlasciviously. In this way you offer her the opportunity to either scream, 'No thanks!', goodnaturedly, or meekly to murmur 'All right', in which case you will obviously have been given the so-called green light.*

Coping with Overt Desirability

Q. I am an unmarried fifty-year-old writer about to move into a cottage in Devon where I had hoped I would be able to finish a book. I have learned from my landlord that the local population of divorced women is girding itself up for my arrival and I am to be inundated with invitations. How can I alienate them at a stroke without being rude?

C.T., Chagford

A. *Word would soon get around if you were to place an advert in the local newsagents giving a clear clue to your identity and simply stating, 'Bachelor, recently moved to Chagford seeks companion. Caucasians need not apply'.*

Q. I am a comparatively small trainer without an Arab owner. I fear that the main client I have will take her horses away if I do not follow up her lightly veiled hints that she finds me physically attractive. What should I do?

N.H., Newmarket

A. *Provided that your prowess at training is undoubted, there should be no reason why you should not employ the following measure and still keep on the horses of the woman you mention. Bear in mind the old dictum: never complain, never explain. Then, at a chosen moment, confide in your owner that you are eternally grateful that your chosen profession consumes so much of your time and energy. 'I have a problem with women,' you can admit. 'Always have had, always will, according to my doctor.' Then, grim-facedly, you can change the subject, leaving your owner to use her own imagination as to exactly what your problem might consist of.*

Bad Breath

Q. I quite fancy a certain person with appalling breath. He seems to like me but I can never stand talking to him for very long because of the fumes. I don't know him well enough yet to say anything. F.W., W.11

A. *Why not employ the trick practised by those on the diplomatic circuit? Blow gently outwards through your own lips while limiting the intake of air through your nostrils during conversational interchanges with such people.*

LONELY HEARTS' DIFFICULTIES

Q. I stupidly answered an ad in a lonely hearts' column and sent my photograph along with my address to the person who was advertising. It turns out that he literally lives next door to me and I have seen him and don't fancy him. What on earth am I going to do when he rings the bell?

G.C., S.W.1

A. *The childish but simple expedient of pretending to be your own twin can be employed. Smiling brightly and politely as you answer the door, say, 'Georgia's my twin – don't worry, everyone confuses us. She's staying with David at the moment. Do you know David, her former fiancé? Well they're back together. I'm rather pleased of course because he's my husband's twin brother.' This last comment should ensure that he does not direct his attentions towards you instead.*

SUDDEN INCREASES IN
PERSONAL EXCITABILITY LEVELS

Q. I don't know what has come over me, but in recent weeks I have been quite unable to concentrate due to a sort of non-specific, undirected sensation of physical excitement. I am twenty-five, surely too young for the menopause, which could account for surging levels of hormones. How else could my libido increase so suddenly in this way? I am unattached romantically and worry that I shall be driven to behave in an unsuitable manner if the sensations do not stop. What do you advise? M.W.S., Berks

A. *Have you been washing your underclothes in biological detergent by any chance? This simple explanation has been found by many correspondents to have solved the mystery sensation of their having 'ants in their pants'.*

How can I stop my friends from chatting throughout my wedding ceremony?

WEDDINGS

THE NIGHTMARISHNESS OF ORGANISING even a small conventional wedding will be attested to by anyone who has ever undertaken the role. Before we look at the multiple hitches and hurdles that will inevitably hinder the first-timer as she goes about her mini-Geldofian task, cringing already in mental anticipation of the piercing embarrassment to come, let us look at the more positive aspects of the day itself.

There are many wonderful things about a wedding day and many reasons to believe that a bride will look back on it throughout her life with memories of unclouded happiness.

Among the pleasures she can look forward to undergoing on the day itself are.

1. Paying back a lot of people to whom she owes hospitality in one fell swoop.
2. Receiving wedding presents from certain of these people (see problem entitled 'Chasing up late wedding presents').
3. Looking as attractive as it is possible for her to make herself.
4. Being pampered by hair and make-up artists, their fingers driving confidently and relaxingly as they go about their work.
5. The emotional joy of union with her partner.
   (Some people also enjoy being the centre of attention but this is variable.)

Set against these good points, a bride can expect the preparation period in the run-up to her wedding to be clouded by a certain degree of dread and fear. The following areas hold rich potential for the realisation of her worst nightmares.

THE INVITATIONS LIST

Who to invite? This is a major problem and mistakes made here will have long-lasting repercussions. A bride-to-be will find that people whom she had previously ranked as nodding acquaintances in fact consider themselves to be among her best friends. Equally, she will find that rancour may be induced amongst workmates who fail to receive invitations. The sort of person she dimly recognises in the lift, who occasionally says,

'Have a nice weekend. Goodnight,' may suffer sensations of rejection on failing to receive an invitation.

GETTING OUT OF ASKING PEOPLE WHO DESERVE TO BE ASKED

Q. Is there any tactful way of not inviting to my wedding people who expect, quite reasonably, to be asked? I am restricted in the number of people I can have and in an ideal world would give preference to people whom I like above those whom I have known longest and who deserve to be asked.

L.F., S.W.1

A. *A woman's wedding day is supposed to be the happiest of her life, yet, ironically, it is often spoiled for her by considerations of emotional debt. There is a dishonest method of dealing with your problem. Perhaps in the circumstances it would be forgiveable to employ it. Write out invitations to all those people whom you do not wish to attend and have the envelopes franked by franking machine in the office post room of a friend. Six weeks later, on or about your actual wedding day, have the same friend reintroduce them to the office postal sack. No Briton will be surprised to receive first-class mail six weeks after it was posted and by this means those who should have been asked will have been asked, yet too late to attend.*

The Controlling of Chatter During the Service and the Speeches

At some weddings the background of buzzing chatter rises to intolerable levels, increasing in volume until it reaches a crescendo, as in the schoolroom. And perhaps it is the very similarity of the scenario to a schoolroom – a large audience commanded to pay attention to one speaker – which encourages the resurfacing of childish urges to undermine authority. No amount of hissing from other guests will stop the talkers in their disruptive tracks; it will only egg them on.

STOPPING GUESTS FROM TALKING DURING THE CEREMONY ITSELF

Q. How can I keep the noise down during my forthcoming wedding? During many of the so-called society weddings I have recently attended, people have carried on talking almost at full pitch throughout the ceremony. During one in particular, at St George's Church, Hanover Square, I noted that Nigel Dempster, who had brought a Watchman into his pew to follow the racing, even turned the volume up when hymn singing began to drown out the commentary. V.H., S.W.6

A. *One way to control friends during a wedding ceremony is to introduce an element of tension. Either you or your partner should appear to be distraught and trembling as you make your way up the aisle. You may even feign a partial collapse. Falter and stammer throughout the vows as though unsure whether to go through with them. You will be guaranteed a totally silent audience, rapt and intense on the edge of its pews.*

STOPPING GUESTS TALKING THROUGHOUT THE SPEECHES

Q. I do not know which to dread more – the speech my husband's best man intends to make at the wedding which will undoubtedly be embarrassingly unfunny or the increasingly loud drone of conversation which I know will very shortly begin to drown him out. He will be using a microphone but even this will not be sufficient to enable him to compete with five hundred voices braying at lecture level. The real problem is that the best man in question is extremely short in stature. He has failed to turn this to his advantage by developing his persona along Napoleonic lines and so the drowning out of his speech will aggravate his existing inferiority complex. How can I shut people up?
M.D., Richmond, Yorkshire

A. *You should employ a two-pronged attack. In the first place the ushers must be instructed that their secondary but no less important role will be to position themselves strategically throughout the mob during the speech-making procedure. Indeed, clear diagrams of their exact posts should be issued along with their pew placement cards. It will be the ushers' duty sternly to approach conversational ringleaders and halt them in their stride.*

As a secondary measure it will be necessary for you to order some especially sticky marrons glacés to be confected by your caterer. These should be served as unconventional

accompaniments to the champagne offered for the toasts.
They will ensure the complete co-operation of your
audience as five hundred immobilised jaws struggle silently
to process the mounds into swallowable consistencies.

PAYING THREE TIMES MORE FOR THE HIRE OF A MARQUEE THAN IT WOULD COST TO BUY ONE OUTRIGHT

One of the great iniquities of life is that it costs three times more
to hire a marquee than to buy one. Why don't people simply
buy them then? Usually because they can only find marquee
hire and not marquee purchase in the yellow pages.

STAG NIGHTS

The tradition of having a 'last night' where the groom-to-be
behaves in a life-endangering manner is still upheld in many
circles.

The correct protocol for stag night behaviour has in recent
years been that the young groom should consume liver-damag-
ing amounts of alcohol, risk death by drunken driving, and
possibly have full intercourse with a paid prostitute – sometimes in front of a cheering cabal of drunks. Few men wish to
take part in such proceedings, yet they are naturally anxious to
succumb to peer-group pressure.

Q. I have heard that my husband's best man is hiring a prostitute to attend his stag night. How can I prevent him from
'doing it'?   C.F., W.11

A. *Why not intercept the prostitute in question as she makes*
her way into the stag party and pay her off. Then step into
the costume which you will have purchased earlier in the
day at a sex shop – a blow-up woman's body, punctured and
ripped at the back so that you can step inside it like a space
suit. Cut holes for the eyes, nose and mouth.

Thus clad, you can present yourself as the prostitute
hired for the occasion and claim through the muffling and
disguising tones of your plastic mouth that there must have
been some misunderstanding with whoever took the book-
ing. You only ever do 'blow up body work' and your boss

told you that this was what was required. Therefore you insist on wearing the costume throughout.

The 'stag' who booked you will no doubt be too confused to argue and you may enter the party. In the unlikely event that your husband-to-be will find the 'body' attractive and make a bid for intimacy, there will be no harm done. He can gain the admiration of his peer group at the same time as you are ensuring he is not laying himself open to any dangerous diseases.

The above are the main sources of anxiety for those who are planning a wedding. Yet the importance of correct timing for a wedding is often overlooked.

Drinking at lunchtime serves as a stupefacient to most people and so it will be necessary to avoid an early wedding, particularly if one is to have dancing later that evening.

One suitable solution is to have the wedding at 5.00 and allow the guests to attend it in ball wear. The wedding should end at 6.00 and then it will be only a matter of time before it is 6.30 and guests are back at the reception. Drinks can be served and dancing and supper can commence.

CHASING UP LATE WEDDING PRESENTS

Q. I am rather miffed because quite a few people who came to my wedding, and were wined, dined and danced at some expense to my parents, have simply not sent me a wedding present, despite the fact that I circulated my list to everyone who was invited. How can I jog people's memories without actually asking them directly?　　　　B.S., Edinburgh

A. *The phenomenon of not giving wedding presents is now widespread. 'I don't want to just get them something off the list,' guests aver. 'I want to get them something special.' This generally serves as an excuse for getting nothing at all as one can never find anything special enough (or couldn't if one had had time to look) and once a certain amount of time has elapsed it becomes too late ('too embarrassing to give them something now'). One method of recovering one's dues is to ring the answerphones of errant guests saying, 'It's frightfully embarrassing but the shop has completely messed up my list and I've got no idea who's given me what.*

85

Would you mind telling me what you gave so I can sort it all out? You must think I've been terribly rude not to have written to thank you.'

GETTING OUT OF BEING MARRIED ALTOGETHER

Q. I am supposed to be getting married next month. Everything has been arranged by Party Planners, invitations have gone out and all the food and drink, marquees and bands have been organised. My problem is that I don't want to get married. I could just about stand the scandal of calling it all off but cannot face telling my fiancé as it would really hurt his feelings. Therefore I am probably going to go ahead with it and get divorced shortly afterwards unless you can suggest an alternative course of action.

C.H., S.W.6

A. *There is still time for you to go down with ME, thus necessitating a postponement of the wedding to an undecided future date. In the meantime why not have a perm? This foolproof means of making oneself unattractive should help to soften the blow to your fiancé and indeed may even precipitate his own withdrawal from the match.*

DIFFICULTIES WITH MARITAL PARTNERS

MANY PEOPLE FIND THAT provocation from their marital partner is the greatest single source of annoyance in their life. Yet to plump for a legal dissolution of the match is generally inadvisable as this tends to involve the wastage of a considerable amount of the accumulated assets of the duo concerned. Lawyers fees are often gross and one partner may well have to sell various prized possessions in order to make cash settlement on the other. New and separate living quarters must be sought and furnished, and invariably both members of the former partnership find themselves in reduced circumstances. Children of such unions would, of course, prefer their parents to stay together and for them to stop arguing, though arguing is, paradoxically, a healthy sign as it shows that the two are still identifying with one another.

TYPICAL ANNOYANCES

A CARELESS HUSBAND

My husband must be the most annoying man in Scotland. I have now bought him three of the most beautiful navy turtleneck jumpers in six-ply cashmere and he has lost all three of them. What happens is that he goes off on fishing holidays with other men and, when he is packing up to come home, just picks up any old navy jumper, usually one worth £19.99 from Marks & Spencer, while another equally careless man will walk off with the six-ply worth £325. It seems completely petty to chase up the other men who were with him to see if they have his jumper and so as a result we have effectively lost a total of £915 over the last few years.   A.MacO., Fife

AN ENVELOPE-SMUDGING WIFE

My wife has one of the most annoying habits I have ever come across. She addresses envelopes in fountain pen and then, instead of licking the stamp, runs it under the tap on the grounds that she might lick up germs from the post office counter, across which the stamps have invariably been 'slid'. As a result, extra spots of water often get on to the envelope and smudge the address. Do you think this irritating?

G.P., Hungerford

A HUSBAND'S INACTION LEADS TO REGULAR BURNING
Ever since we moved into our new house two years ago my husband has been promising to move our heavy double bed to another position in the room, but he has never got round to it. As a result, each time I pass hurriedly between the end of the bed and the radiator in order to answer the phone when I am in the nude, I burn my hip on the radiator. I find this absolutely maddening.   L.M.B., Prague

AN ANNOYING WIFE
My wife comes down every night before dinner looking quite feverish. Her face is generally bright red and in evening dress one can see that her back and arms are similarly enrouged. She generally feels dizzy and faint, and, as she takes her seat by the fire with her gin and tonic, she says, every evening, 'I've had my bath too hot again.'

M.K., Wilts

This representative selection of complaints would seem to suggest that most marital partners have maddening habits. It is both instructive and interesting to consider that each and every person has their own unique method of annoying the person with whom they are in close domestic contact. Let us go on to examine some typical matrimonial difficulties.

TYPICAL DIFFICULTIES

A HYPOCHONDRIACAL HUSBAND
Q. My husband is what a doctor might call polysymptomatic. Almost every day he tells me that he is 'feeling a bid odd' or that he thinks he 'must be going down with something'. The symptoms range from sore throats, feeling blocked up, feeling queasy, or just feeling 'generally run down'. The other day he complained that his eyelids seemed to be fluttering involuntarily. None of the symptoms ever turn into full-blown illnesses and he always refuses to go to the doctor on the grounds that he is going to 'wait and see how this develops'. How can I convince him that he is a hypochondriac as he gets frightfully angry if I suggest that this is the case?

J.F., Balham

A. *Why not keep a diary for, say, a month, in which you dili-gently record the diurnal symptoms from which your hus-band believes he is suffering. After a month you should approach him with the solemn suggestion that he see a doc-tor as there is clearly something wrong. Offer him the unique record you have been compiling, showing the fasci-nating daily progress of the 'disease', and suggest he show it to his doctor. This may serve to nip his complaining in the bud.*

A WIFE DEVELOPS AN OFFENSIVE HABIT

Q. My wife has developed a disgusting new habit of 'belching' loudly. She has always been very horsey and down to earth but this is really extremely unattractive. The problem is that she does not believe that it is unattractive and says 'better out than in'. I have never felt the need to 'belch' myself, so I am unable to demonstrate to her just how offen-sive it is. What should I do?   C.S., Ampleforth

A. *Why not buy a supply of Coca-cola and quaff it hurriedly before meals? This should enable you to mimic your wife's dyspepsia in horrific manner.*

THE PROBLEM OF PROJECTION

Q. My problem is that I have quite simply gone off my wife and feel very little for her now other than a sense of pity. My close friends, in whom I have confided, think I must have gone mad as my wife has never looked more beautiful nor been so successful in her chosen line of business. If any-thing, they say, she should be going off me as I have put on a considerable amount of weight over the last year and my main business, of dealing in antique medals, has virtually folded through my own mismanagement. I, however, feel that the relationship has stagnated and it is time for me to move on. My wife is still in love with me but do you agree that, in a relationship, you must follow your instincts and do what you sense to be right despite their being no rhyme nor reason to it?   E.B., Hoylake

A. *On the contrary, I think you must examine the possibility that you are suffering from the well-known marital syn-drome of projection of inadequacies, whereby the partner with something wrong with him or her projects the defects on to the other. Just as a baby thinks it has no separate identity from its mother, so the partner who may be experiencing 'troughing' with regard to the outside world can confuse his or her lack of adequacy with the state of the marriage. A 'bad marriage' is a convenient scapegoat to which a range of personal failures can be attributed. As you say that you feel pity for your beautiful and successful wife, it seems that you may indeed by suffering from projection-of-inadequacies syndrome. Why not go away for a few months (on medal business) and see if distance does not enhance your perception of the real problem?*

NAGGING

Since babyhood many British men have become accustomed to the reassuring drone of a woman's nagging voice. They therefore deliberately provoke nagging because they like to feel someone is taking an interest in them. If this were not the case, men would not require their wives and girlfriends to nag them by behaving in openly foolhardy manners.

GUILT OVER NAGGING

Q. My husband is a Conservative MP. The one thing that spoils my relationship with him is the fact that I have to nag him perpetually. I have once or twice made resolutions that I will stop it altogether, despite what the consequences might be, but then I see him leaving his keys on the roof of the car or stepping out into Oxford Street with his wallet sticking out of his back pocket and I am unable to prevent myself from saying something. Of course this results in his snapping, 'Stop nagging me woman!' Should I stop nagging him and let him deal with the resultant disasters? Or should I hire a separate member of staff for the sole purpose of nagging, in order to release me to concentrate on purely pleasure-giving interaction?   Name and address withheld

A. *It is unlikely that you could delegate your nagging to a member of staff, even one hired especially for the role. It has been well observed that Britain is a nannyocracy, that many of our leading Conservative politicians were brought up by strict and scolding nannies and that his explains their subjugation to Mrs Thatcher. Yet East Enders along with Etonians will also seek out, and find for themselves, a nag as romantic partner. Yes, an Englishman actually requires his wife to nag him. It makes him feel secure, that someone is keeping a careful eye on him and that he is really still a little boy. His wife or girlfriend is only fulfilling a role which he has set her up to act out.*

DRIVING DIFFICULTIES

Q. My wife and I find each other's driving intolerable. Many journeys have been rendered hellish for me by her heckling and claimed superiority in route selection. When she is driving, however, we proceed with dangerous and uncomfortable spurting movements. We cannot afford a chauffeur, nor can we afford to travel in two separate cars. What can we do about this?   N.L., Fulham, S.W.6

A. *Why not drop in at your local driving school and enquire if they have any dual-control models which they might be prepared to sell you. Possession of such a vehicle could well lead to a settling of your difficulties.*

How can I lose 2½ stone in two weeks?

PERSONAL DEFECTS

Two general points about personal defects come from John Gross's *Oxford Book of Aphorisms*:

How much easier to make pets of our friends'
weaknesses than to put up with their strengths.
Elizabeth Bibesco

Never speak ill of yourself, your friends will
always say enough on that subject.
Talleyrand

MANY OF OUR MOST SUCCESSFUL social figures have learned that having a defect such as cellulite or meanness can actually pay dividends. Far from alienating others, certain defects can serve to promote popularity and generate more invitations than would be forthcoming were the same person to be defect-free.

Apparent perfection of physique, morality and lifestyle are paradoxically less likely to boost a person's invitability quotient. Though such perfection may be admired, it is not so often enjoyed.

On the other hand, the person with one or two glaring but interesting defects, to run alongside his or her capacity to otherwise attract, provides a useful social service. He or she provides scope for amusing interchanges between mutual friends. And more. Gossip is, after all, essentially a moral discussion. If someone allows his or her defects to progress to comic levels, he or she will actually afford friends not only material for their own conversational repertoires but also allow them a three-dimensional yardstick against which they can set their own defects.

Physical defects are, of course, popularising. The girl with cellulite will have far more invitations to beach holidays than the one without.

I would like to quote again from John Gross's *Book of Aphorisms*:

> *He that considers how little he dwells upon the*
> *condition of others will learn how little the*
> *attention of others is attracted by himself.*
>
> Dr. Johnson

UNWARRANTED SENSATIONS OF INADEQUACY

A TYPIST'S TRAUMA

Q. I am twenty-six but I have never got my act together as far as
a career is concerned. As a result I am currently working at
a Battersea estate agency, typing up property details. I have
recently been going out with a much older man who is a
publisher. So far we have just gone out to restaurants like
Kensington Place and San Lorenzo but now one of his
friends has asked us both to dinner at his house and it seems
all the other guests will be really successful media people.
There will be only ten of us and the others will include Mel-
vyn Bragg, Philip Howard, Frank Delaney, Liz Calder,
Hermione Lee and someone called Susannah Clapp who is
apparently really powerful. How can I prevent them from
asking me what I do? I do not want to tell a lie but I would
feel so inadequate admitting that I am only a typist in an
estate agency. Should I pretend to be a researcher?

L.d l B., S.W.11

A. *A little-known fact is that many people in the media have
few, if any, friends outside of it. I can assure you that
nothing would fill the* dramatis personae *you mention with
more gloom than the idea of meeting yet another media
junior. Provided you are reasonably personable and physically attractive – which I presume you must be to have excited the interest of the publisher you mention – nothing
could whet their jaded appetites more than to meet a real
typist who made no apologies for being one and who had no
ambition to be in the media herself.*

SENSATIONS OF PERSONAL INADEQUACY

Q. I used to be quite a figure on the social circuit, but since I
had my three children I cannot help feeling that I have
become desperately dull. Nothing much happens in my little
world with the children in Norfolk, except occasionally a

contretemps with a plumber or some such. I read a lot but somehow I have become inadept at the brittle and immediate sort of chat so essential if one is not to feel inadequate at the occasional London gallery or restaurant opening which my husband requires me to attend with him. How can I engage people's attention for a resonable length of time without a grounding in up-to-date London-based drama and scandal? And what can I say instead of, 'I am a housewife', when I am asked, 'What do you do?' B.E., Holt

A. *Many finishing schools coach pupils in a technique for disguising intellectual inadequacy and you may employ it here. Based on the theory that social agreeability is only a matter of gratifying the egos of others, they encourage the development of a rippling all-purpose laugh, to be discharged virtually continuously throughout all conversations and preceded only by the most minimal of comment.*

The trick is obviously in the timing. This tried and tested technique which has proved helpful to so many others can be coupled, in your case, with the wearing of a mysterious facial expression to suggest that there is more to you than meets the ear.

Few people will resent being faced by an apparently intelligent, if silent, audience of one who seems to be finding them deeply amusing.

As for the problem of describing your role, you should say, 'Oh I do one or two things in Norfolk, nothing interesting'. Follow this with another rippling laugh and then redirect the questioning.

Alternatively you could describe yourself as a 'woman househusband'.

WORDS ON TILES

Q. I keep having to look up the same three or four words in the dictionary. Although I feel I understand the definitions as I am reading them, I find myself returning to the dictionary for these self-same explanations only a few weeks later. The words involved are hegemony, hagiography, behemoth and shibboleth G.W., Macclesfield

A. *Commission your local potter to knock up some tiles to be incorporated into your bath surrounds with the words and their definitions clearly imprinted. Constant exposure to these definitions will enable you to recall them at will.*

Deserved Sensations of Inadequacy

Occasionally certain defects can actually be a turn-off and it may be necessary to cover them up to ensure that one can 'ride out' phases of psychological sluggishness when one may not have much else going for one other than a reasonable physical appearance.

CELLULITE

Q. To put my problem frankly, I look very attractive with clothes on, but I am repulsive undressed. I have an elegant upper body with slim arms and a 22-inch waist, but my legs are virtually the same width all the way down and are pocketed with cellulite. What should I do when required to strip for the beach at a forthcoming holiday in Thailand?

I.C., Kensington Park Road, W.11

A. *Why not pretend that you have had a leg wax which went seriously wrong, and that, under doctor's orders, you must protect your skin from the harmful effects of sun and salt water. In this way you can afford to display the enticing upper part of your body while keeping the disfiguring tree-trunk legs concealed under a cool and lightweight garment such as a sarong.*

COVERING UP THAT ONE IS MASSIVELY OVERWEIGHT

Q. My husband is having some bores to shoot duck on the last weekend of February. He has organised people to come in and help because he knows I can't stand shooting hoorays. For this reason I don't feel I can object to one person in particular who will be coming with her husband. I have not seen her for about five years. My problem is that I am eleven stone at the moment and know that she will go back and tell everyone what a frump I have become. How can I lose 2½ stone in two weeks? Lady D., Scarborough

A. *Do not try. Simply spend the weekend on a day bed, swaddled in rugs and pretending to be in agony with a ricked back. If the extent of your bulk is still discernible, then you*

should retire to your bedroom with a simulated burned leg.
There hospital-style caging, used to protect the injured limb
from painful chafing by the bedclothes, can be improvised
with a fireguard to disguise the entire lower region of your
body.

INABILITY TO CONCENTRATE WHILE RECEIVING DIRECTIONS

Q. My boyfriend and I go away almost every weekend. As we
are both hopeless at map-reading we always have to ask for
directions. We find, however, that although people are
always happy to give directions, neither of us can take them
in as we are so busy smiling and nodding at the very kind
person helping us. This means that we usually arrive at our
destinations tense and late. What should we do?

G.M., W.11

A. *If people know the way they are usually delighted to tell a*
stranger – perhaps because it reminds them of when they
were at school and knew the answer. But many lost Britons,
like yourselves, direct their energies into composing facial
expressions of understanding and gratitude, rather than
digesting the intelligence being given. Carry a pen and pad
in future and ask your guide to write down the instructions.
Then you can smile and nod while they do so.

DISCIPLINING FRIENDS WHOSE DEFECTS HAVE GONE OUT OF CONTROL

Criticism is never well received, despite the fact that, like a
dose of castor oil, its benefits are usually visible within twenty-
four hours.

Nevertheless, the person who metaphorically administers
the dose will remain linked in the mind of its recipient with resentment. For this reason it may be best to mask one's identity
when eking out disciplinary measures, which should, of course,
only be eked out for the long-term good of the defective friend,
who would otherwise run the risk of a drying-up of invitations.

**TIPPING FRIENDS OFF THAT THEIR CLOTHING IS
UNATTRACTIVE**

Q. A colleague and friend of mine has bought a range of what I can only describe as jodhpur skirts – tiny waists, flared at the hips, then in again just at the knee – in the erroneous belief that they flatter her pear-shaped figure. It is clearly the duty of friends to tip her off that these purchases have been a hideous mistake, but none of us in the office likes to do this. Not only has she made a considerable investment by buying eight of the skirts in varying colours, but she is also incredibly touchy and would no doubt 'take agin' the messenger who bore the bad news.   H.de St W., Edinburgh

A. *Why not send a 'perfumed pen' letter? An anonymous, but well-intentioned missive is often the best method to use when tipping off people about defects in their appearance. Without mentioning it to your colleagues, simply type the words, 'You should stop wearing those jodhpur skirts. Signed, a well-wisher', and post this missive to your colleague's home address. She will no doubt puzzle publicly over the letter's content. Friends will be prompted to say, quite ingenuously, 'How weird. Actually I must say the skirts don't flatter you that much but even so . . .' After about four such interchanges, the message will have hit gently home.*

DEFECTS LINKED WITH BEER CONSUMPTION

Q. My husband has decided to plant an orchard at a house we have in Northumberland and I have agreed to go up there with him for a couple of weeks. The problem is that, when he is engaged in 'thirsty work', as he calls it, he insists on having beer at around six o'clock every evening. Though he can drink any amount of wine and whisky without becoming unpleasant, beer makes him a monster. His face takes on an expression of malevolent contempt and he starts to lay into me with insidious and cruel provocation. It always ends up with me in tears. How can I prevent him from drinking beer? He insists that I am imagining he is behaving badly.
L.W.S., S.W.3

A. *Why not buy one of the new Panasonic 'Camcorders', which cost only £899 and can whirr unmanned and unobtrusively in a corner of a room, operate on autofocus and require no artificial light for internal filming. This way you could capture some of your husband's most wounding moments for rescreening on your very own television set the following morning. This measure should be most effective in curbing his excesses.*

LUX FLAKES ON ONE'S HUSBAND'S SHOULDERS

Q. My husband insists on washing his hair in the bath. This means that the shampoo is never fully dislodged as his rinsing method involves him merely ducking his head once under water contaminated by dead cells and soap. As a result he tends to have large clumps of detritus in his hair and on his shoulders. Needless to say, he refuses to change his habits. I can brush the flakes off his shoulders but find it well nigh impossible to deal with the individual pieces of detritus attaching to each hair 'shaft'. What do you suggest?   M.B.J., Cork

A. *Why not purchase a 'Microvac' hand-sized vacuum cleaner as advertised in the* Innovations *report given free with the* Sunday Times *magazine. This neat gadget is promoted for the purposes of sucking dust and unwelcome particles out of cameras and typewriters but will prove equally effective in eliminating the unsightly detritus attaching to your husband's hair shafts.*

NASAL WASTE

Q. Help! What do you do when an intellectually bright fifty-four-year-old male picks his nose publicly and, worse, occasionally eats it!! As a close friend (female), it not only upsets me (I have told him this), but I am deeply embarrassed when other people see the spectacle. Nevertheless, he does it in almost a fanatical frenzy if he is nervous or under stress. What to do?   I.B., Aston Clinton

A. *The public dislodgement of nasal waste is profoundly repellant to a wide section of the populace. Its consumption is unforgiveable. Why then do so many Britons persist with the habit? The simple reason is that perpetrators generally perform the atrocity semi-consciously. They are also unaware of the visual offence given by their actions.*

A considerable degree of success in curbing the habit in a certain well-known social figure was effected, however, by his wife using the following method. Working in collusion with a society photographer who was present at a certain gala dinner, she arranged that a sequence of twenty photographs be shot from long range, which followed the husband's movements closely. When he was presented, at a later date, with a limited edition (of one) booklet in the manner of American flickograms, he was sufficiently horrified to be on his guard against repeating such actions at any later date in a public place.

How can I prevent my sister-in-law from snooping through my personal papers?

PUNISHMENT

MANY PEOPLE TAKE THE harsh step of just dropping friends whose defects have reached intolerable levels. Rather than attempting verbal reprimands or minor disciplinary measures against the offender in question, they choose instead simply to let the friendship mysteriously lapse. And they do this even after years of enjoyment-giving interaction.

Yet how can one know if one has become socially unacceptable unless clear indications are given by one's closest friends? It is they who must tip off malefactors when corrective measures need be taken before popularity wanes irrevocably.

But it is risky to take the role of messenger who bears the bad news. The repercussions can be that rancour ricochets back on oneself.

When criticism needs to be levelled it should therefore be veiled in some way, or even presented indirectly through a third party with one's own link in the chain heavily disguised.

PUNISHING PRETENSION

Q. I have a friend who is hopelessly 'minor public school' and his pretentiousness thoroughly embarrasses all my friends and myself. How can I best approach him on curbing his transparent excesses? I remain your obedient servant.

J.H. de C.S.

A. *Charges of arrogance, pomposity and overt hoorayness are often levelled against those who have attended minor public schools. One practical method of drawing your friend up sharply might be to make repeated telephone calls to his place of work at times when you know he will not be present. Speaking in a thick guttural accent, you should inform the message-taker, 'It's 'is Dad,' or 'It's 'is Mum,' depending on your sex. Eventually, in perplexity he will quiz his secretary as to what the caller 'actually said'. Once told, it may dawn on him that he is being gently reproached and that he should curb his excesses before a more drastic punishment is enforced.*

HALTING AFFECTED LAUGHTER

Q. Someone in my office has a fantastically annoying laugh. It is a sort of scream followed by what sounds like sobbing and is obviously an affectation. How can I stop the girl from doing it without incurring her resentment?   M.W., W.1

A. *Try telephoning her at her own home late on three consecutive evenings. Say nothing by way of introduction, but simply give as good an imitation as you can manage of the screaming and sobbing. The experience should be harrowing and should cause her to think long and hard about switching to a more acceptable form of laughter.*

CONCEIT

Until only very recently it was rather refreshing to come across a conceited person. The trend for several decades had been towards self-deprecation so that there was a novelty value in meeting the occasional renegade who chose instead to communicate a feeling of self-satisfaction.

Now, however, the tide has turned. Too many 'New Positives', their personalities reshaped by assertiveness training and positive thinking manuals, have begun to crowd the pitch.

While one would not wish these people to reverse into modes of negativia and self-doubt, there comes a time when relentless optimism and swaggering self-promotion reach unacceptable levels.

UNDERMINING THE CONCEIT OF A FELLOW WORKER

Q. So many women suffer from lack of confidence that it seems churlish to complain when one in particular develops a surfeit of self-confidence, yet this is the case with one of my colleagues and I'm afraid I am not alone in thinking it. She used to be a rather diffident, sympathetic figure, eager to please and a good listener, but since she has been going out with a certain record producer she has become rather punchy and aggressive and is always bragging about which men in the office fancy her. How can I quell her conceit?

A.O'S., W.1

A. *One careful comment only should be enough to start the spiral of deflation. 'Yes,' you should agree insidiously, when next she brags about being fancied. 'He really fancies you – he always defends you.'*

PUNISHING AN OVERTLY POSITIVE THINKER

Q. I am finding it increasingly difficult to come to terms with a colleague who has recently joined, in a senior managerial capacity, a small business on whose board I sit. It is not so much his perpetually grinning, gnomic countenance to which I object, but that he has obviously been on one of those Positive Thinking courses of which Americans are so fond. This means that, when unpalatable facts and figures are brought to his attention, his eyes seem to glaze over, his visage becoming even more maniacally beaming, while he simply distorts the disadvantage into an advantage.

I might say, for example: 'Our profits are down by 20 per cent on last year.'

He will reply: 'Yes and isn't it exciting that we've done so much better than our closest rivals? Their profits are down by 23 per cent on last year. I really do think that's something we can be proud of.'

What is particularly irritating is that my fellow board members are so frightfully impressed by him. With typical English passivity and mental laziness they are happy to sit back and let him tell them everything is marvellous even when the figures show quite clearly it is not.

How can I force him to rebalance his judgement?

A.W., W.11

A. *You might consider releasing – to coincide with genuine developments in the business – a spate of parodic memos which have supposedly issued from the Positive Thinker's office and which can be 'signed' with the aid of a signature, simply snipped off the bottom of a genuine memo and repositioned on the parodic one. The photocopying process will gradually eliminate the 'joins'.*

Place them on the desks of staff members while the offices are empty.

In these memos you can address topics such as office theft. 'I should like to announce some extremely good news.

105

We have had a spate of handbag thefts in the office. This means that in future staff will be much more careful about leaving valuables lying about.' Or, 'I take great pleasure in announcing the resignation of one of our most valued members of staff. His departure means that our company will once again come into the public eye as we shall be placing recruitment advertisements in all the business sections of the national press.'

In this way you can subtly draw public attention to his excesses. This should not only cause your fellow board members to reappraise his assessments of developments; it may also cause the Positive Thinker himself to consider a less maniacal mental attitude towards business.

PUNISHING EGOTISM

Q. How can I gently tip off a friend that she has become far too egotistical? When she rings up (we rarely actually see each other because she lives in Hampstead, I live in Chelsea) I feel as though I am simply being used as a sounding board while she bangs on about her own life – literally for minutes at a time without drawing breath or allowing me a chance to say anything.   M.L., S.W.3

A. *Next time she actually does pause for your comments, allow twenty seconds to elapse while you make spluttering sound effects from your end. Then say, with uncritical emphasis, 'Sorry, I was using my mouthwash. It only takes ninety seconds and I didn't expect you to stop talking so soon.'*

PUNISHING SNOBBERY

Q. Due to the sudden deaths of two rather distant cousins, I find myself quite unexpectedly with a title, though very little money to go with it. What I find appalling is that certain of the more pushy women in my village, who have ignored me for years while I was an apparently penniless cottager, are now making social overtures towards me. How can I deal with them in a deft and decisive manner?   B., Prestbury

A. *One method of meting out punishment to such people might be to respond to their overtures as follows: 'How nice of you to get in touch . . . I was thinking of getting in touch with you as a matter of fact, because I've come into quite a bit of*

money and I'm going to be able to afford some help about
the house. Would you be available to spare me a couple of
hours a day at £3.50 an hour . . . ?

NAN
I hope I may amuse your readers by relating a little method
which my wife and I use to punish my mother for her ludicrous snobbery. We are basically a middle-class family,
but my grandfather was ennobled by Lloyd George, so my
mother is an Hon. My wife, on the other hand, although untitled, comes from squirearchical stock and is, therefore,
theoretically grander than my mother. What we have done
to tease her is that we have trained our two daughters, aged
two and three, to call her 'Nan'.   A.T., Coombe Bassett

Unhelpful Shop Assistants

The concept of offering 'old-fashioned service' in a shop or
store is once again gaining some credence – as a general con-
comitant of the nostalgia boom. Regrettably, few of the assistants available to work in such stores are of an age to remember
when the motive of a helpful shop assistant was genuine. Instead, their approach tends to be rather artificial in its nature
and they appear as actors playing roles.

There are, however, many shops in the provinces where old-
fashioned service can still be had – where purchases will be
wrapped with vigour and attention, as though the contents
were of extreme preciousness, and where one may even be
given a little loop in the string through which one can put one's
finger to aid the carrying process.

Regrettably few 'unponcey' shops offer such services and it
seems that only the gentry and bourgeoisie can take advantage
of such service. And they pay for it. As one shopper commented
when he left the butcher Wainwright and Daughter on the Fulham Road in London, where old-fashioned service presided,
'You're paying for those stupid nodding puppets in the
window'.

In far greater abundance exist those shops where new-
fashioned service is the order of the day. Most of us are familiar
with the insolent unhelpfulness we encounter when entering

such establishments: 'If it's not on the shelves, then we haven't got it'.

Q. I patronise our only local video hire shop reluctantly. Not only is there an inordinately large 'Michael Ryan' section for such a lovely rural backwater as Clare, but I find my stress levels rising as I attempt to deal with the youths who tend the till. They carry on talking amongst themselves when one is obviously waiting to be served. But worse, they give that most maddening of replies when one asks for help; 'If it's not on the shelves then we haven't got it.' What can I do to bring them up sharply?   W.A., Clare, Suffolk

A. *The following method of dealing with unhelpful 'assistants' can often be salutary. Take your intended purchase to the counter and pass it across for wrapping. When the assistant drawls out the price – '£2' for example – you should reply languorously: 'If it's not in my pocket, then I haven't got it'.*

PUNISHING ROUÉS

Q. I was recently surprised to find myself the object of intense and sudden passion from someone I had previously written off as being a rather ludicrous, though very good-looking roué. As his campaign gathered momentum I began to feel rather flattered. Eventually I capitulated to his demands. It was with intense embarrassment that I discovered, through using his answer-phone call recovery system which he had left in my flat, that a bet of £1,000 had been at stake between him and a fellow roué as to whether or not a conquest could be effected. A friend has suggested I should type a letter to the Inspector of Taxes, purportedly from him, declaring the income and enquiring whether or not such winnings are subject to betting tax. Do you feel this would be a suitable punishment?   M.S., S.W.1

A. *No, it smacks too much of sneaking to the authorities. A more suitable course, in my view, would be to make nuisance phone calls to his answerphone on a nightly basis for two weeks.*

There will be no need for you to identify yourself or to leave any spoken message. You will need a recording of a song called 'Bohemian Rhapsody' by a 'group' named

Queen. *Even a snatch of this song will plague the consciousness of anyone who hears it for a full day. Any of its climactic choruses can be played from your end to nightmarish effect. Two weeks will be more than enough to punish him.*

PUNISHING NOSINESS

It is the most natural thing in the world to wish to examine the contents of another person's bathroom cabinet when one has finished making use of facilities there. As surely as night follows day, the inexorable route taken by the hand of a normal person spending time in a strange bathroom will be: tap, water, soap, towel and bathroom cabinet.

This form of nosiness cannot reasonably be condemned. However, prying through drawers, filofaxes, and laundry baskets is quite a different matter and deserves punishment.

PUNISHING A SNOOPING HOUSE GUEST

Q. I have rather reluctantly agreed that my husband's sister may use our flat in London for a weekend while we are out of the country. I have always suspected that she has tendencies to snoop and am particularly concerned about the contents of the desk in my study which does not lock. How best can I set a trap to catch her out and let her know that I am on to her game? L.B., Penzance

A. *Prior to leaving your London flat you should drop into a junk shop and make a purchase of a simple box-like wall cabinet made in any sort of cheap materials and measuring roughly two feet by one. A catch of only minimal sturdiness should be incorporated into the design.*

Lie the cabinet on its back on the floor of your study and fill it to capacity with marbles bought from any toy shop. Lock the cabinet door and affix the cabinet firmly to its wall mount that a builder has prepared for you. Use a drawing pin to affix a small notice saying 'Private' to the front of the cabinet.

In this way, should your suspicions about your sister-in-law be correct, the evidence will be incontrovertible.

Punishing Inefficiency on the Part of One's Agent

Q. I would like to get across a message of dissatisfaction without having personally to deliver it. I am seething with resentment over the inefficiency of my literary agent. First, he hung on to a royalty cheque for two years, thus losing me considerable bank interest. Then he failed to negotiate a contract for my latest book until after it was published. I do like him very much despite this but feel he should not get away with it. The trouble is that I have always hated any sort of confrontation or unpleasantness.

Name and address withheld.

A. *Arrange for your agent to receive an angry letter from your mother demanding explanations for each of the acts of inefficiency. Allow sufficient time to elapse so he can reply to the charges. Then telephone your agent to convey your embarrassment, saying, 'My mother has always been very eccentric. I'm so sorry, she must have been going through my papers'.*

A Stinging Punishment

Q. Everyone seems to be taking themselves so seriously these days, what with this new money mania. I wish I could find a way of getting people to laugh at themselves again as they used to before Thatcherism really took off. Can you think of anything? C.O.

A. *I always find it amusing to have a nettle planted in an indoor flowerpot at one's place of work. People are invariably drawn to touch it, murmuring, 'What's this unusual plant? Looks rather like a nettle.' Though childish, it is nonetheless gratifying to be able to reply, 'It is a nettle,' when they are stung.*

How can I tell whether or not my daily has been using my telephone to ring her family in Brazil?

STAFF

THE DYNAMICS OF A SUCCESSFUL master and domestic servant relationship are little understood. Many wonder how one person could be willing to clean up after another. And so they consistently demoralise their dailies, robbing them of the satisfaction they might gain from their work, by doing it themselves before the dailies arrive.

Such people underestimate the satisfaction to be had from performing simple physical tasks and from bringing order and thereby a degree of happiness to the life of another. More importantly, when one works as a daily, there is visual evidence of what one has done with one's time. By contrast, estate agents, stockbrokers or bankers will find at the end of an eight-hour stint that they have been battling with a many-headed hydra. As one loose end is cleared up another one manifests itself with frightening immediacy. Thus any achievement they might make is masked from them, and their mental turmoil is never reduced, always level-pegging.

For dailies, butlers, and certain nannies, there is an additional psychological relief to be gained through working in back-up capacity to another person. May I refer to the experience of one fashion-leader who once held a position as a type of lady-in-waiting to another more powerful woman.

It was a loosely defined role in a loosely defined decade, the 1970s. Essentially, however, she fulfilled the functions of factotum and general involvee in all aspects of her employer's life. As intimate observer of the aforementioned, she was able to offer informed, though detached, advice on the always dramatic, sometimes harrowing events of her employer's days as a leading *femme fatale.*

Taken up completely by her employer's life, there was little opportunity to dwell on her own. Living vicariously, she gained detached pleasure from the triumphs in which she had obviously played a part, yet suffered minimal distress from the disasters. She reported that it was like having a holiday from herself, and was immensely relaxing.

Vicarious-living facilities are a key factor in attracting and sustaining the interest of staff who are willing to work in subsidiary support systems. The ultra-grand Rospigliosi Bureau in London's West End, which supplies staff to many of our well-known stately homes, has often surprised its clients by acquiring for them super-efficient young butlers of similar, sometimes higher, social rank to their own. Generally, staff, of course, are notoriously hard to come by.

DAILIES

GETTING A DAILY IN THE FIRST PLACE

Q. My husband and I have just moved to a property near Stow that has been in the family for years but was until recently rented out as a girl's school. It is a most attractive house but it seems impossible to find daily help in the area. Some of our neighbours do a 'daily run', but it is a round trip of sixty miles and I am loath to take part. I fear we may have to move back to London. What do you suggest?   J.J., Glos

A. *In areas where the merest thatched hut just off the motor-way is occupied by millionaires, the old adage 'first come first served' has a peculiar relevance. Dailies who can still afford to live in such areas have all been bagged long ago by indigenae and new property owners can only hope to lure them into service by offering the going London rate of £4.50 per hour. Advertisements should be placed offering this figure but on no account should dailies be poached from friends or acquaintances.*

SECURING FULL-TIME ASSISTANCE AT ONLY £13 A WEEK

Q. Can I train a lady's maid as part of the Youth Training Scheme and thereby save myself a fortune in wages?

S.R., Amersham

A. *Positions on the YTS have to be open to anyone, regardless of their sex. If you are happy with a male maid and if your household, as a training ground, meets with the approval of the 'work experience placement officers' at your local social services, then the scheme may go ahead. You will pay about £13 a week for your maid, who will also be expected to do a day release course once a week at the local polytechnic. If a course in domestic service does not exist in your area, then the council officials may be unable to help you.*

CHATTY DAILIES

Q. How can I make it clear to my daily that I cannot spend an hour each morning bemoaning the disasters of the previous day with her? I don't wish to appear inhuman, but now that there are so many disasters each week, I find that discussion of them eats quite considerably into the time that she should spend cleaning.　　　　　A.B.,Campden Hill Square, W.8

A. *There is nothing you can do about it except be out or busy with the papers when the daily is present. However, one employer claimed to have had success by inventing an old superstition: 'Never discuss a disaster. 'Twill being another one faster'.*

PHONE-MILKING BY DAILIES

Q. My telephone bill has trebled in the quarter since I engaged a new daily who comes from Brazil. I don't want to accuse her without being absolutely sure, yet how can I catch her when I am out all day?　　　　　Q., W.11

A. *Make a point of going home one day while your daily is at work. Push the last number redial button on all your extensions. On connecting with Brazil, say 'Espere un momento, por favor,' and call the offender through.*

Chucklingly explain that a Portuguese speaker has answered the telephone at your best friend's house and you cannot get the message across that you want to speak to him. Say, 'I know it's the right number because I was speaking to him last thing last night and I have just pressed last number redial'.

Smile pleasantly and thank her for her helpfulness as you force her to talk to the other end.

NANNIES AND MONTHLY NURSES

Living with people whose 'wavelength' differs from one's own can cause disharmony to reign in a household. Nannies who are unhappy with their figures, for instance, or their complexions or their lack of a romantic partner, may often transmute feelings of personal dissatisfaction into feelings of bitterness against their employers. Teenage nannies are particularly prone to view themselves as victims of injustice and cruelty perpetrated by their bosses.

Unbeknown to their employers, nannies can nurse unreasonable resentment along with their charges for many months before suddenly turning on their startled bosses with a tirade of accusations. They will then 'walk out' triumphantly.

As it is inconvenient and unnerving to have a constantly changing retinue in one's nursery, it is preferable to arrange that grievances are aired as and when they arise, so that they can be dealt with at an early stage. Yet nannies are notoriously unforthcoming about grievances, storing them up in silence until their cup runneth over and their only course is to leave.

There is a step you can take to avoid this happening. Nannies should always have their own telephone line. In this way you can keep a check on their 'real cost' by paying the standing and hire charges yourself and an agreed amount of the billed units. You can also keep a check on their personal happiness by occasionally plugging in the baby alarm under nannie's bed and then eavesdroping on her calls from downstairs.

If grudges are rehearsed on the telephone – and many of them may be valid – you can always approach nanny the following day, saying that you had left the alarm on in her room by mistake and could not help overhearing her call. You are sorry she is unhappy. How can you put it right? And in future, will she please tell you if there is something wrong?

Not all nannies are troublesome. Many are life-enhancing.

GETTING A CHEAP MONTHLY NURSE

Q. I am expecting a baby but simply cannot afford to pay a qualified monthly nurse the going rate of around £170 per week. Is there any way around this?   J.G.

A. *Put an advertisement on the noticeboard of the coffee-room at New Zealand House off Trafalgar Square. Many fully qualified nurses from that country pass through London and, desperate for accommodation and money while in England, they are willing to give up a month of their time to take up such a position at the greatly reduced figure of £50 a week.*

STOPPING NANNY AND HER BOYFRIEND FROM SLEEPING IN ONE'S BEDROOM

Q. We have engaged a little nanny from Newcastle who is absolutely charming and very good with our six-year-old. Nanny doesn't work at weekends and we usually leave her to house and cat sit while we go down to the country. I know she has a boyfriend and wonder how I can prevent them from sleeping in our double bed while we are away.   M.A., W.11

A. *Tell nanny that, as you have most of your jewellery in the bedroom, it has been wired with an independent alarm system to that of the rest of the house. 'It's terribly complicated so I won't bother to explain it to you,' you can say as you leave for the country, 'but I've left it on so just make sure the cats don't get in there as the slightest thing will trigger it and set alarms screaming all over the place.'*

LEGITIMATE PROBLEMS OF NANNY'S OWN

Q. I am working in this country for six months as a nanny to a lovely couple with beautiful homes in the Cotswold country and right in central London, in the Chelsea district. They have two sons, a baby of three months and a six-year-old little devil who is making my life a misery. He tells his parents I have hit him when I haven't, that I have given him boxes of matches to play with and various other lies you wouldn't dream a little child could make up. Worst of all, he comes up to the nursery and says, 'I'm going to get you into trouble now,' and tells me what he is going to say. I want to keep the job but I am sure his parents would not believe me if I told them the truth. What can I do?   Z.T., S.W.3

A. *Why not leave the baby alarm plugged in during one of these interchanges so that his parents can hear for themselves?*

IMPROVING THE QUALITY OF ONE'S LIFE BY LIVING IN A RICH PERSON'S HOUSE

Oddly, very few people consider this instaneous method of making themselves physically comfortable. The houses of rich people, even those of formerly rich people, can be relied upon to offer the following sensuousness-raising agents: crisp, clean linen sheets; thick, clean, rough or smooth enormous bath towels, scalding hot running water, light-filled rooms with crackling real fires and beds and chairs of heavenly comfort and, in country houses, fresh organic produce from the garden.

Why then do not the down-and-outs in Cardboard City flock to take up positions in such households? Thousands of stone-built, art-filled palaces, set in beauty spots from Land's End to John O'Groats, are occupied by one solitary old person who, *faute de* being able to get someone – anyone – to come and live in, has to sell up and move into a nursing home.

Employers should be cautious, however, of applications for domestic positions made by obviously suspicious characters such as gold-diggers who may try to marry them (see page 137).

STEALING A COUPLE

Q. I have not spoken to my cousin for some years since he stole a couple from us. We have never been able to replace them successfully. How does one go about it?

S.W., Pershore, Worcs

A. *It is best to put your name on a metaphorical waiting list. Make enquiries amongst your friends as to whether any of them has an ageing relative currently looked after success-fully by a couple who can be warmly recommended. The legatees of such people are usually vastly relieved to think they can offer alternative employment to the faithful servants of their relatives on their demise.*

OTHER PROBLEMS WITH STAFF

Non-domestic staff can give problems of their own. The most common problem suffered by top-ranking male personnel is that of imagining they are in love with their secretary instead of their wife. This condition results from a form of egotism. The secretary is witness to all her boss's most impressive moves throughout the day; she is also up-to-the-moment on all the mini-dramas which take place during his working hours. She can therefore discuss these with him and it soon begins falsely to appear that the 'couple' have a lot in common. In reality, the only thing they have in common is that the secretary, with her shared references, is able to offer the boss sounding board and team-member sensation, which will no longer apply when they marry and she ceases to be his secretary.

PROBLEMS WITH OVER-STAFFING IN A PUBLISHING HOUSE

Q. For some years my husband has been running a small publishing house. He has been reasonably successful but our
profits are severely eaten into because he is wildly over-
staffed. The problem is that he is very kind-hearted and has
given positions to the children of friends who want to get
their foot in the door, kept jobs open for people who have
had babies for years on end, given jobs to ne'er do wells,
drunks – in fact virtually to anyone he liked and who
wanted a job. All these staff members are blissfully happy
and not one of them is ever likely to move as their jobs are so
pleasant and conducted in the most cosy environment. My
husband cannot bring himself to sack anyone and so it looks
as though we are facing ruin. What can I do?

J.A.D., N.W.3

A. *Why not persuade your husband to make his office open-
plan and install fluorescent lighting. Open-plan offices are
suitable for time-servers and workers in duller jobs where
the only stimulation to be had is from manwatching. However, sensitive people, such as those who work in publishing, generally find the open-plan system personally dimin-
ishing, intrusive and uneasy-making. Should the dreaded
fluorescent lighting also be installed, it should not be long
before resignations start to flood in.*

HOIST BY ONE'S OWN PETARD HAVING SUCKED UP TO A WORKMAN

Q. I have made the mistake of being too friendly and patronising towards a workman who has been doing some invaluable
repairs around the house. He keeps hinting that his wife
wants my husband and me to come to dinner. How can I get
out of it when he asks directly? A.B., S.W.11

A. *Simply say, 'We never accept any invitations to spend time
with other couples who don't swing. We have been into the
whole wife-swopping thing for so long now that we always
get carried away and start to come on to the other people
present. We find we regret it the next day. It's better to
simply say no.' This way you cannot hurt his feelings.*

TRAVEL

TRAVEL CAN BE EXHILARATNG. Its most important facet is to offer a holiday from oneself. For this reason travel has been less satisfactory in recent years, as people have found more and more explicit and three-dimensional reminders of their life at home wherever they venture in the globe. Chiantishire in Italy is, of course, the most ludicrous example of this phenomenon. But it is equally no longer an amazing coincidence to meet someone you know from home in Papua New Guinea; it would be rather more amazing *not* to meet someone you already knew from home in such a far-flung venue.

Now holidays in such difficult places as Bhutan or Vietnam are resentfully undertaken by would-be fashion leaders. Meanwhile, the real fashion leaders are seeking out experiences in such obscure and unspoiled (by lesser fashion leaders) districts as the Orkneys, Cornwall and the North Suffolk coast.

Long-distance travel throughout Britain has now become the absolute norm for many socialisers on typical weekends. Helicopters and planes are employed by those who can afford them to get to the most distant points from London on weekends but, for many, the motorway journeys comprise at least one-quarter of the hours they spend 'relaxing'.

GAMES

Q. Can you suggest any amusing games to help pass the time during monotonous car journeys? I am driving to North Wales next month in a Renault Espace with four friends.

K.W., S.W.12

A. *Why not play 'The Shortest Distance' game? The quizmaster, who changes with each round, gives the names of two friends or acquaintances who are at least vaguely known to the other occupants of the car. The idea is to work out the shortest distance between these two people using others with whom they have been 'romantically linked' as stepping stones. The contestant who links them with the least number of go-betweens will win the round and will then be entitled to pose the next question.*

Going Bananas Trying to Remember Who Someone Is

Q. I am thirty. I was on the train the other night, from Paddington to Exeter, and there was a man sitting across the gangway from me whose face I knew extremely well. He was a rather distinguished-looking, thin man in a suit, aged about sixty-three, and he was reading a rather obscure book on ecclesiastical architecture. I longed simply to say to him, 'May I ask your name?' But he was clearly of an irritable disposition as he kept wincing when other people in the carriage used their portable phones, so I did not dare. As a result I had to disembark at Westbury, feeling quite dissatisfied, with the riddle still unsolved. What should I do if I see him on the train again?   C.L.G., Westbury

A. *If you are travelling in a carriage full of people with portable telephones it should be possible for you to approach one of these types and whisper the request that you borrow their telephone for a thirty-second experiment which will not involve your actually notching up any units. You may then approach the irritable stranger and, holding the telephone at a mysterious angle as though there were, curiously, a call for him, simply say, with your brow furrowed in puzzlement: 'Excuse me – may I ask your name?' As there are new and astounding developments in technology every week, no Briton will be surprised to learn that he has been tracked down in his train carriage by some sort of new computer and, caught off guard, he will almost certainly give his name.*

At that point you can say, 'Oh I'm sorry, the call's not for you,' and move back to your seat with your curiosity satisfied.

Potential For Entrapment of Eligible Bachelors on a Sleeper

Q. I know I am going to Scotland by sleeper on the same day as a boy I really fancy. I feel that there must be some way in which I could use this journey time to further our relationship. Can you suggest anything? L.R., W.11

A. *Call the sleeper enquiry number at Euston (071 387 8541). Say, 'My husband has already made a reservation for himself on (say) the 7th. I'd like you to make it a twin berth as I'll be accompanying him.' Then give your would-be suitor's name (let us say he is called Lochinvar).*

'Certainly Madam,' they will say. You should then go to a travel agent and pay for the booking in cash.

Three days later, by which time Euston will have confirmation that the booking has been paid for, ring them again and say, 'Mrs Lochinvar here. I'd like to cancel my sleeper reservation for the 7th but my husband's cousin will be accompanying him instead so will you simply switch it into his name? Don't bother about a refund. His name is Russell'. (This, of course, is your own name.)

On the night in question, arrive at Euston early, dressed in masculine garb. Enter your carriage. Your names will be pasted on the door: Berth 14F Mr Lochinvar; Berth 14G Mr Russell. Quickly get into bed and pull the covers up.

Once Lochinvar himself is installed and the train has started to rumble through the night, you can stir sleepily from your berth. 'Good Lord, I don't believe it,' you can say. 'What are you doing here? I didn't know they had mixed compartments!' As you travel a good deal of enforced intimacy can be achieved. You marvel together at the coincidence and, if Lochinvar is so inclined, he may feel that fate must somehow have masterminded the mix up and that your destiny as romantic partners is clearly indicated.

GETTING OUT OF GIVING LIFTS FROM THE AIRPORT

May I offer you some advice about what to do on an aeroplane with a new friend/acquaintance when you know your car is at the airport (short term/long term/flyaway parking) and they have not got transport to London and they live north (not very) and you live marginally south. The problem is how to get out of giving them a lift honourably. This happened to me recently on a flight from Aberdeen. Frankly we were just too tired to give this very nice girl we had met a lift to north London. So I went to the telephone saying, 'We're supposed to be having drinks/

dinner/lunch with someone. Let me go and just ring them and see if they are running late, because if they are we can give you a lift home. I then returned saying "I'm afraid we have to go immediately. They are waiting for us".'   S.M., S.W.10

SPALLING

Q. Now that we have good weather in England, how can I prevent myself from 'spalling' in the bright sunlight. I find that I come home from holiday after two weeks of continuous facial grimacing with a whole new host of wrinkles each year. Worse, they are wrinkles whose existence is highlighted by the fact that they are unsuntanned.

I.B., Bakewell

A. *It may well be worth your while to consult optician Tony Gross of Cutler and Gross, 16 Knightsbridge Green, and purchase a pair of his wrap-around Aristotle Onassis sunglasses which are totally U.V. absorbing and which will prevent the glare from penetrating from side angles.*

Telephones

FAR MORE THAN THE TELEVISION, which might be said to have actually soiled our perception of the world, the telephone is the great pleasure-giver of the communication revolution. Though data is relayed in an equally artificial manner over the telephone, it is received by an active rather than a passive mind.

The man in the long coat running over the fields may have been replaced by the more instant deliverer of bad news, but, as we find ourselves in the position of having a great percentage of our favourite people moving to other ends of the globe, is it not an under-acknowledged source of ecstasy to be able at least to talk to them if they have made up their minds to go there anyway?

Nonetheless, many Britons, particularly those under the pressure of having rounded up too many friends, or having taken on too ambitious a business venture, find the telephone a source of threat.

THE BEST MESSAGE TO LEAVE ON ONE'S ANSWERPHONE

Q. What is the best all-purpose message to leave on one's answerphone so that one has the option of either picking up the calls as they come in or dealing with them later?

R.M., S.W.10

A. *How about 'I'm either not here or I'm pretending not to be here. Please leave your message, speak after the tone.'? This way callers will be flattered when you break through their message to talk, but will not be offended by your failure to do so as they will have no means of knowing whether you really are there or not.*

On the other hand, it is not just the receiver of a call who feels threatened. It can be equally threatening to have to make a call to a friend who may be chairman of a bank, Press secretary at 10 Downing Street or managing director of the Royal Opera House. One would be glad if an answerphone were to pick up one's message in such scenarios, so that the object of communication could ring back at a moment which was not inconvenient. The tremble in their tone, once one has reached such people, often indicates that one has called at the wrong moment – very few moments in their day could possibly be the right moment – despite the fact that they have given you the number of their direct line when they were drunk.

For this very reason, the fax machine has become invaluable for dealing with power-brokers. There is no need for time-consuming pleasantries such as 'How are you?' or 'By the way, I meant to thank you for dinner the other night, it was really lovely. I really enjoyed meeting blank etc.' One can move straight on to the business in hand.

For example: FAX
    FROM: GABE DOPPELT
    TO: GERRY FARRELL

Loved dinner. Thank you. Please fax me the name of the tailor who made your green jacket.

This, as opposed to:

'Hello. May I speak to Gerry please?'

'May I ask who's calling?'

'Gabe Doppelt.'

'Can you hold the line please?'

Thirty, forty, fifty seconds . . .

'Gabe?'

'Hello darling. 'I can tell you're busy . . .'

'I'm always busy, but never too busy for you, Gabe. Now, how can I help you?'

'Oh I feel guilty for ringing you at work, Gerry. Shall I ring you later?'

'Of course not, what was the nature of your query?' (said impatiently but with good humour).

Gabe laughs (taking up fifteen valuable seconds). 'I just wanted to say thanks for dinner.'

'It was lovely to see you.'

'And, I'm sorry to bother you at work but can you give me the name of the tailor who made your green jacket?'

'All right, hold on, I'll just look up his number for you. Ruth? Ruth? Hold on a second Gabe. Ruth, where have the phone books gone? All right. Gabe? Hold on a moment, Ruth has just gone to get the phone books.'

'Oh well, let her tell me the number. I'm sure you're

busy.'

'There's no problem, just hang on. Oh, no I don't believe it. Can you hang on a minute, Gabe, just hang on there's someone on the other line.'

Three, four, five minutes go by.

'Gabe? I'm so sorry. I had to take that call'.

'Who was it?'

'Someone I'm supposed to be meeting in Germany in about three hours.'

'No! Look, I'll get off.'

'Please don't. It's always a delight to hear your voice.'

'Oh, no, I'm going to hang up now. Please, just give me the number when you next see me.'

'I wouldn't dream of it, I'm just about to find it. Now, tailors . . . Scott Crolla, Johnson & Johnson, Gieves & Hawkes . . . Listen Gabe, I'm going to have to ring you back. I can't find the number for some reason.'

'All right, lot's of love.'

'Lots of love.'

Crack.

For this reason, the fax is invaluable. For those who are not in possession of a fax machine, yet need to make reasonably urgent contact with a figure from the corridors of power, the correct procedure is as follows:

Forget you have the number of the direct line to your desired communicatee. Instead, ring the main number of his household or place of business and ask for his secretary. Having got through to the secretary, say, 'I know Gerry is busy. Can I just leave a quick message with you? Thank him very much for dinner and ask him if he would give you the number of the tailor who made his green jacket. I'll ring back in an hour and you can tell me what it is.'

PROBLEMS SUFFERED BY THOSE WHO CANNOT GET OFF THE TELEPHONE

Q. I have got to the stage where I dread answering the telephone as I find it virtually impossible to 'get off'. Even when I sense the other person would rather like to get off, too, I find myself dragging out the threads of the conversation in case they should feel hurt by not prolonging contact with them to its fullest possibility. What can I do?

F.B., Ridgewell

A. *Interrupt the preliminary interchanges of all telephone conversations by barking, 'Hello? Hello?', while your inter- locutor is still speaking. 'Sorry,' you can lie, 'the phone's playing up again. We've had them round to fix it but it's no better.' When you have finished transmitting all necessary messages, embark upon some piece of trivial gossip then simply put your finger on the cut-off button while you your- self are speaking. Most callers will not bother to ring back.*

GETTING OTHER PEOPLE OFF THE TELEPHONE

Q. How can I avoid the long and unwelcome calls I receive about twice a day from someone I cannot be rude to, but who likes to ring up and use me as a sounding board while she bangs on about her own imaginary problems?

M.W., S.W.11

A. *Why not keep an old-fashioned tin cup by the telephone? Minimise your own greetings to all incoming calls so that on hearing from your unwelcome caller you can instantly raise this muffling agent to your lips and announce. 'This is a recorded message. Sorry we are out at present. Please leave a message after the tone.'*

USING THE TELEPHONE AS A MEANS OF GETTING AWAY FROM SOMEONE

Q. What I find irritating about the telephone is that it never rings when you want it to. I often pray for it to ring at times when someone from the village drops in and is prolonging the conversation unnecessarily. Can one arrange to have alarm calls, say every ten minutes, so as to give one an ex- cuse to get away from people? C.L.G., Liskeard

A. *Yes it would be possible to receive such calls but it would also be grotesquely expensive and inconvenient. A far more suitable method would be to ask a friendly telephone engineer for the code number which he uses in your area to* test whether the bell on your phone is ringing correctly. It is usually a four figure number but it varies from area to area.

Having once ascertained what the number is, you simply pick up your phone, dial the four digits, and put it down again. Immediately your telephone will ring back.

So, for example, if you are trapped in your kitchen with your neighbour, you simply say, 'Just excuse me one second.' Racing from the room you go quickly to a nearby phone and dial the four digits. Put it down and come quickly back into the kitchen. 'Oh no!' you can say, turning on your heel to answer it. After thirty seconds or so of 'talking' you should come back into the kitchen and say, 'I am sorry. I'm going to be some time on the phone.' At this moment your neighbour will seize the chance to say, 'Well I must go anyhow,' and will make her way gratefully out of your house.

GETTING PEOPLE OFF THE PHONE BY USING THE METHOD OUTLINED ABOVE

Q. I am the editor of a rather successful periodical. My problem is that the person who 'owns' me likes to feel he takes a hand in the editing of the magazine. As a result he regularly rings me at extremely awkward moments to discuss editorial policy. As he is a rather touchy individual it is hard for me to say I must get off the line now and get on with my work. What should I do?   Name and address withheld

A. *Why not have a secondary line installed in your office, if there is not one there already? When you have had enough of your conversation with your owner, you need simply lift the handpiece of the secondary telephone, and using the method outlined above, ring yourself back. When your owner hears the other telephone going in the background he will no doubt be happy to accept that it is time for his own call to come to an end.*

MAKING FRIENDS WITH THE OPERATOR

May I offer your readers some tips about a telephone service which very few people are aware of? I am a thirty-eight-year-old bachelor teaching at Wadham College, Oxford. I recently had cause to ring the operator to ask for the number of the recorded recipe of the day. While she was attempting to put me through, we struck up a conversation about cooking. I explained what sort of things I had in the house and how I had suddenly realised I had four people coming to dinner in an hour. The operator immediately gave me a suitable recipe from her own repertoire and even stayed on the line talking me through the various stages of the dish, which was, incidentally, tuna and bean tagliatelle.

She explained to me that operators were only too happy to have some sort of prolonged contact with their callers with whom they normally interact for only five or ten seconds.

Since then I have regularly rung 100 for advice on cooking and found the operators extremely helpful. I thought your readers might well be interested to hear of my experience.   G.W., Oxford

LAVATORIES

THE PROCESS OF MAN'S civilisation marches inexorably forward, yet one obstacle to his total freedom and sophistication still remains. Medical researchers and government spokesmen alike are unanimous in their verdict that, so long as human existence continues in its present form, it is unlikely that there will be any significant changes in the pattern of ingestion and digestion of man's foodstuffs.

In other words, it is likely that highly civilized man will continue to experience difficulty in certain social scenarios when the need arises for him to deal with the elimination of waste matter engendered by the food-processing system.

Two basic problems have to be looked at. First, a decision needs to be taken as to how to phrase one's request to be directed towards the waste-processing facilities when one is involved in social intercourse in unfamiliar settings. The second problem concerns concealment of both gaseous and sonorous emissions linked to waste expulsion.

Euphemisms are almost always employed, even by those of no-nonsense outlook, whenever the matter is raised in a social context. People may ask, 'Can you show me the geography of the house?' Older women may ask, 'May I powder my nose?' Sources which suggest that members of the royal family employ the term, 'May I make a royal flush?', are to be taken lightly.

Current euphemisms in use among the sophisticated classes include: 'Which direction do I go in?' 'I must go and settle myself', 'Which way are the heads?' and 'May I use the facilities?'

GENERAL PROTOCOL

Q. What is the current protocol about going to the loo?

B.J., Beauly

A. *In line with many other facets of contemporary life, the business of going to the loo and the customs associated with it have come in for a shake-up. In the hippie generation, liquid relief was gained both in public and in the open air (though solid waste was never fashionably discharged). In the early 1980s it was certainly fashionable (if foolish) to be seen heading into and out of lavatories, but actually needing to go has never been less in fashion. In an emergency you may go in a friend's house but you should never leave the table in a restaurant to make use of the waste facility.*

Q. What should I say when obliged to leave the table, as I regrettably often find myself required to do, during a dinner party in a private home, in order to use the lavatory? Should I say 'I must go to the loo'?   C.C., N.W.1

A. *No, you should simply rise from the table with a mysterious expression on your face and leave the room, issuing no comment either before your departure or after your return as to what you have been up to.*

RUDE AWAKENINGS

Q. What is the correct protocol for one's night-time use of antiquated sanitary systems not *en suite* when staying with friends? Do you crank the ancient machinery and run the risk of waking the entire household or does one leave evidence for fellow guests to find in the morning?

C.B., Ridgewell

A. *A number of unfortunate incidents have resulted from panicking weekenders making use of improvised receptacles and then having trouble disposing of the contents. Crank the ancient machinery at all costs.*

BOMB SURPRISE

Q. I have been invited up to Scotland next month to stay in a party of twenty in a wonderful fishing lodge. I am devastated to hear, however, that my so called 'best friend', who knows I have been madly in love for a year with one of the men who has been invited, has asked our hostess to put her in the bedroom next to him because she fancies him. They are the only people in the same corridor and are even sharing a bathroom. He is incredibly shy and is the sort of person who would start going out with anyone who was in the next bedroom to him and made a pass at him. What can I do to prevent it?   K.F., S.W.11

A. *I always feel stink bombs are massively underused in these circumstances. They can be bought from any trick shop and all you need do is nip into the shared bathroom every so often and drop the tiniest suspicion of the liquid on to the floor. It doesn't matter which one of the pair thinks the other is responsible for the appalling fall-out. Either way it is likely that any potential fancying will be nipped in the bud.*

Chain Lesson

Q. My wife and I have a few friends who use the lavatory in our various houses and always forget to pull the chain. Is there anything we can do to prevent them being so selfish?

A.B., Bradford-on-Avon

A. *I understand a device is available which was invented by the same man who invented and designed Big Ben. This imposes a simple locking mechanism on the lavatory door which cannot be released until the chain is pulled. Your friends will therefore be locked inside until they have behaved more considerately.*

Houseguest's embarrassment

Q. I find it terribly difficult to go to the lavatory in another person's house when I am staying overnight.

J.V.S., Richmond, Yorkshire

A. *Your worry is understandable. In Japan this problem is dealt with by mini tape players which transmit various sound effects from music, to hot air hand dryers, to repetitive flushing sounds. These players are carried into lavatories by Japanese women who keep them about their persons at all times as the Japanese are highly sensitive to any form of embarrassment.*

In England these devices are not as yet available so the best solution is that you should use only lavatories which are en suite with baths. In this way, you can run a bath simultaneously and thereby drown out the evidence of your own perfectly natural activities.

CRIMINAL DISCHARGE

Q. My cousin Jonny was once arrested in Draycott Avenue following a meal at Le Suquet fish restaurant with his friend Tim. The two men had had quite a lot to drink and found themselves out in the street into the early hours when they decided to answer the needs of nature. Unfortunately, they were both arrested on charges of obscenity and spent the night in jail. They were fined the following morning in court. Can you tell me what is the legally acceptable procedure for dealing with such emergencies?   N.H., Stockwell

A. *An ancient bylaw, created for the benefit of coachmen, permits anyone to answer the call of nature in any public place providing they have first shouted out in a loud voice three times 'In Pain!'*

BRONCHO

Q. I miss the crisp old lavatory paper of yesteryear. Brand names such as Izal and Bronco spring to mind. I do not know whether these still exist or whether they are easily obtainable. Can you shed any light on this matter?

G., Portman Square, W.1

A. *Rumour has it that these old brands with their unbleached sheets, the rough texture of which discourages wastefulness, will soon be back on the market to coincide with the boom in green consciousness. In the meantime you may find it worth your while to become a member of the London Library in St James's Square (circa £80 per year) where I understand there is an ample supply of old-stock hard paper.*

The danger that one's aged relative may marry his nurse, thus stripping one of one's rightful inheritance.

MONEY

IT'S GREEN TO BE MEAN

Money is a touchy subject where a lot of people are concerned, particularly when those people have a lot of it. Meanness, however, is currently very much in vogue because it can be easily disguised as an aspect of the fashionable green anti-waste, pro-recycling movement.

Thus the same millionaires who would have provoked raised eyebrows in the recent past if they re-used an envelope, served their guests with left-over food or rushed to extinguish a forty-watt bulb are now being commended for such actions. Best of all, for the budget-conscious, is that they can now give wedding and christening presents of saplings without the recipients daring to comment on the minimal financial outlay involved.

Being mean can be rather an absorbing hobby. When one constantly clocks up how much one is saving throughout any given day by, for instance, going on public transport, not putting the heating on but wearing a jumper, forgetting the chequebook when going out to dinner, etc., the sums saved can very soon begin to seem sizeable. And though meanness is a prime characteristic of many of our most well-off, fashionable and popular social figures, this trait more often serves to provide their friends with anecdotal material than to alienate them. So being mean does have its own peculiar cachet.

MINIMISING OBVIOUS WASTES OF MONEY

PARTIES IN NIGHTCLUBS

A multiplicity of drains on one's resources will arise in the ordinary course of events if one is not on one's guard. Distributing largesse in a private home or marquee is quite different, for example, than distributing it via a free bar in a hired nightclub which one may have chosen as a suitable venue for a party due to its fashionable decor, location or music. In such scenarios guests tend to take 'one sip' of their drinks – usually quite poisonous if the wine is being supplied by the nightclub itself – and then put it down while they go off to dance. Having thereby 'lost' their drinks, guests will go to the bar and get another one and the host will be obliged to pay six or seven times the customary outlay for drinks distributed through this bar system than they would in a private venue. For this reason some millionaires have recently chosen to have pay bars in nightclubs where they host parties, reasoning that, as they paid for the hire of the club and the invitations, these in themselves are adequate in the line of largesse.

SHEET-CHANGING EXPENDITURE

Q. My husband and I live in one of the most beautiful country houses in England. As we are also rather centrally situated we regularly have people passing through on their way elsewhere and staying for one night only. It does seem ridiculous to be constantly dragging off cardboard-stiff, blindingly white bedlinen in order to replace it with 'clean'. Our local laundry makes a killing from us. What do other people do?   A.D., Ramsbury

A. *Many country house owners find it convenient to make a stockpile of the heavy-duty paper bags used by their local laundries for deliveries. These are left conspicuously discarded in guest bedrooms, as though by hurried oversight. Following 'one-nighters' such as you describe, the same sheets, stretched stiffly and tucked tightly under the mattress, may then be reused, though pillowcases should be changed. Even the most suspicious of guests will be duped by the discarded packaging.*

LINEN, A READER WRITES

May I refer to the advice you gave in a recent reply to a country house owner whose constant throughput of overnight guests was leading to crippling laundry bills? I took a particular interest in this case, as I myself am the owner of a conveniently situated house in Kensington and have had friends coming and going for many years in a similar manner. It was not so much the money I resented as the time and effort involved in stripping and remaking the beds. I have recently arrived at a solution which I would like to pass on to any readers who might be interested. My solution is certainly ideal for my own household (which might be described as haut Bohemian) if not for the more grand country house scenario. As I point people to their room, I usually say, 'There are some clean sheets and pillowcases up there'. On arrival in the room, guests see the clean sheets sitting on the bed which is already made up with sheets from the person before. With any luck they are too drunk or too lazy to bother remaking it and simply slip, perfectly happily, into the 'pre-soiled' sheets of the previous guest.

A.C., W.8

AVOIDING WICKED NURSES

Q. What is the best method of finding a live-in housekeeper to look after my ageing father? He is ninety-six and increasingly dotty but insists on staying in our family house in Scotland which is ten miles from the nearest town.

C.A., Dornoch

A. *You may advertise for assistance in* The Lady *or* The Times *but do not mention the fact that your father is a widower. Many fortune-hunters scour the housekeeper-nurse ads for positions with elderly (rich) men with short life expectancies whom they then marry, thus stripping the rightful heirs of their inheritance.*

DIFFICULTIES OVER MONEY WHERE FRIENDS ARE CONCERNED

Some of the greatest anxieties generated over money come about when one's own friends are involved.

Close and adored friends will lamentably, and all too frequently, blot their copy-books where money is concerned. They will go to the loo when the bill is about to arrive for a dinner that a group has agreed to share the cost of; they will move in as a lodger and 'forget' to pay their rent; they will come round in light clothing and ask to 'borrow' a coat to go home in, and never return it.

While the dusty chequebook is most commonly found in the drawers of our most favourably endowed friends, many of us are prepared to write off this minimal annoyance. Yet difficulties can really arise when two friends are in pursuit of the same quarry and sums of money can be the deciding factor over who will win.

DIFFICULTIES OVER BIDDING AGAINST A FRIEND AT AN AUCTION

Q. What is the correct protocol for bidding against one's own friends in an auction room? I often have people to stay with me in the country and many of them enjoy the auctions in our local sales room. If I am interested in bidding for the same thing as one of my guests, should I step down and allow him or her to bid for it, on the grounds that they are my guests? Or should they step down and allow me to bid for it, on the grounds that I am their host?

D.McC., Holt, Norfolk

A. *It would be better manners for your guests to step down as they would not be at the auction were they not accommodated within striking distance of the auction room by courtesy of yourself. When, however, there is an object towards which more than one person in your group feels strongly attracted, then you should put forward the business-like suggestion that you form your own dealer's ring.*

Only one person from the group should bid, to a ceiling agreed in advance. If the object in question should be sold to your group (of three, say) you can split the cost between the three. Once back at your own headquarters you can instigate a second auction whereby the three bid against one another. In this way the person who wants the object the most can express himself by actually offering to pay the most.

The method is satisfying because it means that everyone can gain something. Say the object cost £30 at auction and each of three people paid £10 towards it. Back at your house a second auction shows that one of the three is prepared to go higher than the others to secure the object for himself. He will pay £60.

He gets the object, and is satisfied, yet he must also pay his two rival bidders £25 each to get the object. Therefore, having docked their initial outlay of £10 in the auction room each of the two rivals makes a profit of £15 while the highest bidder gets the object for less than he would probably have had to pay were the object being bidded up by his own friends in the auction room.

RECOVERING LOANED MONEY

Q. I have a very vague friend who regularly borrows small sums of money from me and more often than not forgets to repay them. I don't really mind when it is £5 or £10 as I can write that off against the pleasure I get from her company, but the most recent unpaid loan of £42.50 is rather too much to write off. This was the amount I paid when, as a favour, I picked up a pair of shoes belonging to my friend's husband which had been resoled and reheeled at Jeeves in Belgravia. She was not in when I dropped them off, and though I have seen her three times in the last few weeks, she has not mentioned paying me back, though she did thank me for having collected them. What should I do? I don't know why, but I don't really want to ask her directly to pay me back.

B.L., Milner Street, S.W.

A. *The trick to recovering money from vague borrowers is to affect a certain vagueness yourself. Next time you see that your friend has her chequebook handy you should gasp 'Oh! That reminds me. I must pay your back that £42.50 I owe you.'*

'Really?' your friend will reply. 'What was that for?'

'Oh, it was for picking up some shoes from Jeeves – no hang on a minute. I picked them up – I must be going mad – you owe me £42.50.'

This method of reversal and simulated vagueness can be used with success in collecting all manner of debts to which one is embarrassed to refer directly.

A GODSON WHO HAS NOT THANKED

Q. I sent my godson £25 in cash on his ninth birthday last October. I have heard nothing. How can I find out whether the money ever reached him without embarrassing him or getting him into grouble with his parents for not having written to thank me? I cannot bring it up casually as they live in Surrey so I never see them.

P.E., near Marlborough, Wilts

A. *Write to your godson along the following lines: 'Due to the recent arrest of our local postman, I am writing to ask whether you received the £25 I posted to you last October. Some of the mail he was given charge of was recovered by police officers from a local gravel pit and has been reintroduced into the system. If your letter was one of these you may soon receive it. If not, I must send you another. Do let me know what happens. I enclose a stamped addressed envelope for your reply.'*

MAXIMISING ASSETS FOR LOW INCOME GROUPS

The newly poor can usually coast through for a further generation beyond their impoverishment, and continue to enjoy the concomitants of a millionaire lifestyle courtesy of friends they have made through their family or public school. Thus the reality of penury may often not sink in until such people have reached their early thirties.

DISTRESSED GENTLEFOLK

Q. I stupidly persuaded my trustees to let me break the trust and now I have blown all my money. At thirty-one it is a bit late for me to start looking for a job. Can you give me any information on the Distressed Gentlefolk's Association?

S.G.C.,Oddington

A. *Though anyone can apply to be helped by the Distressed Gentlefolk's Aid Association (and in fact they wait for applications rather than seeking them out), their typical beneficiary is an impecunious elderly person who has 'given public service' and fallen on hard times – for example, the widow of a major-general or even a musician. I got the impression from their spokesman that an application from someone like yourself might be unsuccessful. May I suggest some alternative courses of action?*

I always find that checking the cinema floor can provide one with welcome windfalls. But for more substantial income why not try the method of money making which regularly draws in funds for unscrupulous Americans. A small ad is inserted in a national newspaper with the simple message, 'You owe me £10'. A box number is given. Guilty

people flock to send cash in response to such advertise-
ments.

GUTTER PRESSURE

Q. I have been working for almost a year as a receptionist to a leading London dentist. Among his clients are many politicians and other eminent people to whose dental records I have free access. Could you advise me as to whether there would be any market in the so-called Gutter Press for these confidential documents? S.S., S.W.11

A. *It is unlikely that information about upper-right occulusals and the like would be of much interest to readers of any level of intelligence and anyway the sale of such material would be illegal for ethical reasons.*

PROBLEMS WITH BANK MANAGERS

I felt I must write in and share with you the pleasure I extracted from a recent interview with my bank manager. The fellow had been writing me supercilious letters whose main drift was that my attitude towards money was irresponsible. I invited him round to my flat to discuss a loan I wanted to negotiate. I offered him a sherry and he accepted it. I then said, 'Do excuse me, I'll just get myself some Perrier water.'

'Aren't you joining me in a sherry?' he enquired.

'Good Lord, no,' I replied. 'It's much too early for me.'
This ruse served successfully to put him on an apologetic footing and I was satisfied to be able to negotiate the loan I required. A.F., Islay

A FINAL ANXIETY OVER MONEY

Q. I have never understood a word my accountant says. It is not his fault but mine as I have always been hopeless about jargon. Now I have to register for VAT and must go to a meeting with him so that he can explain the system to me. I understand no leniency on grounds of incomprehension is given by VAT inspectors and I am dreading having to serve a jail sentence. What can I do, short of having my accountant live in? M.K., Wilts

A. *Take a tape recorder along to your meeting with the accountant. Simply pose the questions and sit back and relax as he answers them. You can play the tape repeatedly in your car stereo until the basics have sunk in, then return for final questioning.*

EMBARRASSMENT

IN AUTOBIOGRAPHICAL WRITINGS, Bertrand Russell looked back on a life rich in history-shaping incident. As a central figure at many of the century's key political and social revolutions, as the lover of famous and beautiful women with whom his relationships had been powerful and dramatic, he looked back on the ninety years he had lived through so far, and observed that the strongest and most vivid memories he retained were those concerning incidents in his life where he had been embarrassed.

Embarrassment is absolutely ghastly and, as part of life's rich tapestry, completely unavoidable. Let us look, however, at some of its prime causes in today's society in a bid to minimise its potential horror through education and preparation.

A LETTER WHICH SHOULD NEVER HAVE BEEN WRITTEN

Q. I have just received a ludicrously pompous letter in florid violet ink from a girl of twenty who has married my nephew. The purpose of her missive was to upbraid me for having switched my placement at her wedding reception. I am sure the letter was written in haste and she probably regrets having sent it. How should I reply?   R.McC., S.W.10

A. *Do not bother. Replace the letter in its envelope and smudge the violet ink, as though with rainwater, so as partly to obscure the address. Then hand it in at your nearest post office saying you found it in the street. The post office will stamp it 'Damaged in transit' and, as is their practice, return it to the address of the sender as shown within. In this way you will avoid compounding the embarrassment.*

APPARENT EXPULSION OF 'WIND'

Q. I met with some business contacts for a drink at a hotel in Sloane Street the other night. As I sank into a leather sofa in the bar, the sound of a whoopee cushion was emitted by the sofa itself. As the people I was with were clearly embarrassed, I decided to take the step of continuing to move about on the sofa in order to induce repeatedly the same sound effect. This way, I felt, my companions would realise that I had not personally been responsible. I have since heard, however, that these valued clients gained the impression that I was suffering from some sort of severe digestive disorder and that, as a result, they were rather disgusted by the whole experience of meeting me. What should I have done.?   K.K., S.W.10

A. *Anyone sitting on a leather sofa for the first time should take the precaution of commenting, before sitting down, 'I hope this isn't one of those whoopee cushion sofas'.*

EMBARRASSMENT TO DO WITH PERSONAL HYGIENE

NASAL HYGIENE

Q. Is there a discreet means of determining whether or not one's nose is bleeding? At parties I often suffer from a curious tingling sensation coupled with a feeling of dampness in one nostril. Though the anxiety invariably turns out to be groundless, the process of checking is unattractive.
                                                A.B., Ripe, Sussex

A. *The least offensive method of checking is to blow the nose, then immediately drop the handkerchief on the floor. This ruse will facilitate checking for discolourants during the stooping and rising involved in recovery.*

DENTAL HYGIENE

Q. I once had spinach stuck in my teeth when on an important lunch date as a teenager. Since then I have never been able to enjoy eating with other people as I keep imagining things will be stuck in my teeth. I know there are hypnotic tapes available to help one cope with various phobias but I have not been able to find one which deals with the phobia of having food stuck in one's teeth. Can you help?.
                                                H.B., Co. Westmeath

A. *Why not use your knife as a mirror to make discreet and periodic checks on your dental cleanliness.*

GREETING OTHER BOYS AT ETON

Q. I started at Eton this half and would like to ask your advice

about something. What is the correct protocol for acknow-
ledging or greeting other boys when you sometimes only
know them because they are in the same class as you for
something for three hours a week yet you pass them six or
seven times a day either in the street or in the corridors? Do
you have to keep saying hello each time?   N.B., Eton

A. *The problem of bumping into someone for the 'umpteenth'
time in a day is endemic to all institutions, whether prisons,
holiday camps or art colleges. The key rule is to avoid eye
contact and to this purpose many older boys pretend to be
either drunk or drugged as they pass through the streets
and corridors of Eton. For younger boys, such as yourself,
it is more suitable to pretend to be engrossed in your own
personal reverie, a vague smile playing about your lips as
you walk, staring straight ahead and possibly humming
some favourite tune.*

GETTING RID OF MORMONS
OR JEHOVAH'S WITNESSES

Q. How can one get rid of Mormons or Jehovah's Witnesses
without being rude? Friends say, 'Just slam the door in
their faces' but I simply can't do it. They are frequent callers in the area where I have a small country cottage and, as I
answer the door myself, I live in dread of being 'caught' by
them. This means that I have missed out on visits from
people I actually wanted to see.

                    S.M., Bourton-on-the-Hill

A. *One way of dispatching such well-intentioned but unwelcome callers is practised by a well-known Oxford don.
Interrupting the dogmatising early on, and looking brightly
into the faces, she says, 'Oh, you go door to door, just like
me. I'm an Avon lady myself. I'm sure either you or your
wife would be interested in my products and may I just say
they are the highest-quality cosmetics you will be able to
find on the market. We do something to fit the pocket of
everyone and . . . ,' continuing with a sales pitch of her own.
She found the activists, taken aback by this reversal of
roles, would beat a confused but swift retreat.*

Vulgarity Linked to Polo

Q. Can you settle a dispute between my husband and me? He insists on displaying his Cowdray Park Club sticker in the back window of our BMW and I insist that this is deeply embarrassing. What is your own stance?   S.P., Chelsea

A. *The only car stickers currently acceptable to be displayed by adults are those promoting conservation causes. Motor rally and polo stickers were last acceptably displayed in the 1950s though the Cowdray Park sticker is marginally more acceptable than those stickers available on Smith's Lawn.*

Clapping

Q. I have an anxiety neurosis about clapping. I find it such a peculiar and even primitive practice that I tend to get rather frightened at the end of a theatre performance when I look around me and see rows and rows of people behaving in this almost surreal manner. I can't bring myself to clap and feel guilty that the cast will think I have not enjoyed the performance. What should I do?   M.W., Wiltshire

A. *Most actors and actresses are aware that there is a convention among theatre critics whereby they do not clap. There is no reason why you should not pass for a member of that select group, particularly if you appear to be making notes on your programme while others around you are clapping.*

Embarrassment in the Hairdressers

Q. My hairdresser always says, 'When your fringe gets too long, just drop in and I'll always trim it for you without your having to have a full appointment.' How much does she expect me to slip her in this situation?   M.K., S.W.3

A. *If you are a regular customer, then many salons will see it as a duty to keep your hair in shape between cuts and will perform this service free without expecting you to slip the girl anything.*

Explaining One's Embarrassing Expulsion from a Public School

Q. I have finally succeeded in getting expelled from a frightful minor public school two years and two rustications after my arrival. My parents were very understanding because they regretted sending me there in the first place, but my mother now has to face the task of explaining to malicious and conspiring friends and relatives why I will be working at home until my A-levels next summer. Any ideas?

K.S., Stoke-on-Trent

A. *How about total allergy syndrome? You can always claim to have identified the rogue allergen as something like Quink at a later date when you want to be able to socialise openly.*

Stopping Others Chatting Throughout a Speech Being Given

May I offer you a solution to a certain problem that many of your readers are bound to come up against? In my role as a senior figure in a university, I have been obliged for many years to attend certain board meetings where slightly long-winded and dull speeches are likely to be given.

My problem was how to stop the person next to me from whispering a jocular commentary in a disturbing and embarrassing manner during such speeches, and by his actions, implicating me as recipient of his comments.

I reached a solution, almost by divine inspiration. If I suspected trouble from the person beside me, or, indeed, if it began to arise, I would whisper to him, or her, 'I've heard he (or she) is going to make an extremely complimentary remark about you during this speech.'

This would generally ensure that the offender would, from that moment, sit in a most golden silence beside me, giving no further trouble.　　　　　　　　　　　　　　　　　　E.H., Bangor

How can I prevent my teenage son from sleeping his life away?

SHARED ACCOMMODATION

MANY BRITONS FIND IT NECESSARY to share accommodation for budgetary reasons, yet they also find they can derive deep satisfaction from the camaraderie that sharing can offer, as well as a sense of security from intruders. Live-in friends can be the source of intense happiness for the compulsive socialiser, who can rely on:

1. On-the-spot sounding boards for the purposes of chatter and analysis.

2. Someone else whose wardrobe and social programme one can take advantage of.

3. Someone else's food in the fridge.

Unfortunately, particularly after the age of twenty-five when the first stages of crustiness in the human character begin to manifest themselves, problems can arise. Resentment mounts in three particular areas.

1. Disputes over who has generated the mess and whose duty it is to clear it up.

2. Disputes over who has used the telephone most.

3. Disputes over who has finished off certain foodstuffs, with particular reference to orange juice or Perrier on mornings when each person in the household has a hangover.

An explanation is given in the chapter entitled London Life (page 52) of the importance of engaging a daily when one is sharing accommodation. An ordered and therefore harmonious home environment means that one does not have to go out in costly pursuit of relaxation and one can save considerable sums each week through being able to cook at home. If, however, squalor reigns in the cooking quarters – with unresolvable conflicts over who is to blame – then inmates may be driven out to expensive restaurants on a nightly basis, rather than clear up the squalor and cook at home.

A daily must therefore be engaged, the cost divided equally. Meanwhile, a blind eye must be cast on the disproportionate amounts of squalor generated by each contributor.

Telephones

Now that the Mercury telephone company, rival to British Telecom, is offering itemised bills, there should be no need for dispute over division of the telephone bill. Simply switch your phone on to the Mercury system and you will find your quarterly bill drops dramatically.

Other People Drinking One's Orange Juice

It is the natural and inalienable right of a hungover person to drink an entire litre of orange juice should he open a fridge door and find one within. It would be too tortuous to deny him that. Later on when he recovers he will go out and replace it. That, of course, is not good enough if the person who bought the orange juice has a hangover too, and happens to reach the fridge door an hour later and desperately needs the orange juice himself.

But that's what sharing accommodation is all about.

Stopping a flatmate from wearing one's clothes

Q. I strongly suspect that my sister, who is my flatmate, wears my clothes while I am away for the weekend. The problem is that I cannot lock my cupboard door as the cupboard itself is an antique and our mother won't let us have a lock fitted on it. Also her bedroom is off mine so I can't have a lock put on my door. How can I catch her out or at least stop her from wearing them?   E.Z., Edinburgh

A. *Most expensive stationery stores still stock old-fashioned sealing wax and seals. All you need do, on going away for the weekend, is to heat a stick of wax over a candle, taking care to avoid fire hazards, and apply the so-called blob of wax along a small area of the door frame. Then 'seal' the wax with your own special insignia with which the stationery store will issue you. This means that, if your sister opens the cupboard door, the wax will break. Even if she equips herself with a supply of sealing wax to cover up the fact that she has broken in, she will be unable to mimic the insignia.*

A Delicate Problem of Pilfering

Q. I am a forty-five-year-old bachelor and I have been staying rent-free for almost six months in the very convenient Kensington home of a friend. What is irritating is that his rather brattish eight-year-old step-daughter has been pilfering money from my room while I am at work. Both the girl and I know that my friend would be horrified were I to impute such charges against her and I feel it would almost be ungracious to prove them after the hospitality I have received. What can I do?   M.W., Cambridge Place, W.8

A. *There are two methods by which you may induce the eight-year-old to expose herself. The following age-old method of entrapment should first be attempted. Allow £5 to be stolen from your room, then announce suddenly and casually, as though commenting on your own muddle-headedness, 'Do you know a £10 note has simply vanished from my room?' At this point a guilty eight-year-old will invariably reply, 'It wasn't ten pounds, it was five.' Should this method fail, announce to your host that theft at work has made it necessary for you to buy a rather amusing little Property Marking Kit (available from security specialists at £25.30), with which you now mark every banknote which comes into your possession. Offer to demonstrate the kit and laughingly produce a banknote marked with the kit's ultra-violet pen. Illuminate the marking with the kit's ultra-violet mini-lamp. 'Compare this,' you add, 'to an ordinary note such as one from Little X's piggy bank. Do let us have one so that I can show the difference,' you can plead innocently.*

An Undesirable Lover is Moved into One's Shared House

Q. I am twenty-seven. I was panicked into buying a house with another girl, or rather a woman, of forty-nine, in the run-up to the cancellation of dual mortgage relief. My house-mate, who has not previously been married, went to Morocco on holiday last September, struck up a relationship with a nineteen-year-old waiter and fell in love with him. I was happy for her until she brought him over to England on a nine-month visa to share the house with us. I am now finding his presence intolerable for a variety of reasons. What should I do? I don't want to deprive her of her happiness and, anyway, as she is a co-owner, I have no right to ask her to chuck him out.

R. de la L., N.W.3

A. *You should arrange to rent a one-bedroomed flat in the short term. In the meantime advertise your own accommodation for rental. Hold out for another nineteen-year-old Moroccan waiter. When you have arranged this, tell your housemate, with the pleasantest of miens, that, because you are feeling rather claustrophobic and want to be alone, you are moving out for a few months. A stranger will be taking over your room in the meantime, and by an amazing coincidence, he happens to be Moroccan too.*

DEEP BATHS

Q. I share a flat with three others in Oxford and they are always getting at me, saying that I use too much bath-water. They all have really shallow baths but they don't want deep ones. How can we resolve this problem? It's not as if I'm using all the hot, because it's heated by gas anyway.

M.M., Oxford

A. *Sharing accommodation is often tricky. Why not pretend to comply with your friends' wishes? Run only shallow baths. Then, once the door is safely locked, introduce the shower tap under the water of the bath and supplement your bath-water to your satisfaction without your friends being any wiser.*

LODGERS SNOOPING THROUGH ONE'S PERSONAL PAPERS

Q. My son and his girlfriend live in the basement of my house in Chelsea. I have a strong suspicion that his girlfriend comes up to my study when I am out and snoops through my papers, either to see how much I am worth or simply out of old-fashioned nosiness. In any case, I want to put a stop to it, but for obvious reasons I do not want to seal up the door to the basement. What do you suggest?

A.A., Tedworth Square, S.W.3

A. *While many householders install time-switching devices to their electrical systems to deter burglars, a pre-programmed lavatory flusher would probably be more appropriate in your case, where the 'burglary' is an inside job.*

EMBARRASSING BELLS

Q. I am deeply embarrassed. I rent the top floor of a three-storey house in Fulham and my landlady, who is incredibly 1970s, has labelled the three doorbells outside the main front door as follows – bosoms, waist and then a triangle, to show which bell to press for which floor. I am afraid to say anything in case she is offended, but it is in such bad taste. What can I do?   G.W., Chesilton Road, S.W.6

A. *Why not telephone your local police station anonymously and tip them off that a brothel is clearly being operated at a certain address? When they call round to investigate they will no doubt advise your landlady as to the unsuitability of her bell labels.*

GROWN-UP CHILDREN LIVING IN THE BASEMENT

Q. My husband and I have a basement flat in our house in Holland Park which is lived in by our two teenage sons. We all get on very well and I do not resent the fact that we are, in theory, losing income because we cannot rent it out while our sons are there, but I am just worried that they will never grow up and get married while they can always come up to Mum to borrow food and get their laundry done. Yet London rents are so expensive it would be the most terrible drain on their resources were they unable to live at home. What do you suggest?   A.O'P., Holland Park

A. *I think you should find a suitable bachelor flat for your sons to move into and thereby release your own basement flat for rental at the equivalent rate they must pay out. You can pay their rental for them out of the income you make from renting out your own basement.*

153

Getting Teenagers Out of Bed in the Morning

Q. During the school holidays my teenage son spends most of his mornings hulking away in bed. He is not on drugs, nor is he suffering from depression, but he has taken up some crackpot American theory that he should rely on his own body clock to wake him naturally when he is fully rested and that it is damaging to his psyche to be woken by artificial means such as alarm clocks or the firm voice of a human being. As he manages to hang on to his sleep till almost lunchtime every day, I am getting increasingly frustrated. His young life is sifting away, like the sands in an egg-timer. What can I do? He absolutely snaps the head off anyone who goes near his bedroom, or hoovers outside the door as a way of waking him.   B.O'P., Co. Westmeath

A. *Why not wake your son up by the entirely natural means of birdsong? Many homeowners with suitable facilities for blackbirds in the immediate environs of their territory find that they cannot possibly sleep through daylight hours due to the delightful, but insistent callings of the birds outside their windows. Tapes of birdsong are available in the novelty record section of most large stores. You need simply turn on the tape below your son's window and set it going when you consider he has had enough sleep. Though many teenagers feel they genuinely 'need' thirteen hours of sleep a day, and all over the country, teenagers are hulking away in seemingly impregnable comas at this very moment, your son will no doubt find that roughly eight hours are as adequate in holiday periods as they are in school terms. Even if he is aware of the reason why he has woken up, he could hardly claim that being woken by birdsong was in any way unnatural.*

Q. Can you suggest a job for my rather lazy teenage daughter to do in the three months before she goes abroad for a year? She is very pretty and vaguely wants to be an actress but sleeps until lunchtime every morning. I am in despair.
                                             S.M.N., S.W.3

A. *Why not suggest she approaches the bedding departments*

of London's top stores such as Heal's or Peter Jones and asks for a job sleeping in one of the beds during opening hours to demonstrate its comfort. Such a move would bring publicity to the store and might even entitle her to an Equity card.

A foolproof way of catching a waiter's eye.

Restaurants

ONE OF THE DISADVANTAGES of being a Briton is that our restaurants have less satisfactory traditions than their continental counterparts. Tension is more likely to be heightened than dispelled in a British restaurant, where self-consciousness reigns, waiters ignore one, and bills are extremely frightening. British restaurants make a striking contrast with the gloriousness of restaurants abroad where hours at a time can be spent manwatching in pavement- or beach-side reverie while balmy breezes caress us and olfactory stimulants, such as garlic, coffee and just general foreignness, give to life a heightened sense of vividity.

What is curious about foreign restaurants is that satiation can be achieved more often than not at only marginally more than the cost of buying the same materials and preparing them oneself at home. In Britain, however, only workman's cafes and fast-food outlets are budget-friendly. Restaurants in general purport to offer a treat rather than serve a function and can only be patronised on a regular basis by those on expense accounts or from the upper-income brackets.

Yet, despite their cost and comparative sexlessness, restaurants in this country still serve as backdrops to most of the pivotal social, romantic and business developments of our time. Indeed, the sexlessness of an English restaurant is one of its chief attractions for many major figures from the corridors of power in whose minds pleasure is complicated by its association with nannies.

Nursery Food

This term describes those stodge-based menus enjoyed by traditional Englishmen in London clubs, the Houses of Parliament or private homes lived in by other like-minded men. Roasts, butter-loaded mashed potatoes, and particularly the great British puddings, such as Roly-Poly or Spotted Dick, are typical examples of this cardiac cuisine so popular with fully grown men who loved their nannies. Now, in adulthood, they seek to re-create the comfort that they felt in nanny's company by consuming the sort of dishes they remember from her nursery.

Nursery food is on offer in restaurants such as Wiltons in London's St James's and Green's, opposite the Houses of Parliament in Marsham Street, where a division bell rings to send the MPs back from their fishcakes and bread-and-butter pudding to cast votes. But there are many traditionalists who feel that such restaurants do not go far enough.

A RESTAURANT NAMED NANNIES

May I offer some advice to any restaurant 'backers' who may be looking for ideas for a successful theme restaurant? It has long been my ambition to join forces with nanny expert and author of *The Rise and Fall of the Great British Nanny*, Jonathan Gathorne-Hardy, to devise a new restaurant going by the name of Nannies, where traditionalists who seek comfort from their dietary intake will have their tastes catered for. At Nannies, nursery food would be served and the fully grown diners would be waited on at table by stern women of bulky physique.

Gathorne-Hardy visualises his role as style consultant and insists that such a restaurant should go all the way. Diners would be required to wash their hands thoroughly before eating. And they would find that, if anything was left on their plate, the next time they came to the restaurant they would finish up the leftovers before being allowed to order anew.

Yours, Hugh Montgomery-Massingberd, W.2

PROBLEMS WITH WAITERS

Just as the middle classes are the snobbiest people in the country, so one finds that waiters working in restaurants which charge middle-range prices tend to be the most superior towards their customers.

And in many cases their customers respond by feeling inferior. Indeed, while British women are frightened of their hairdressers, many British men are frightened of waiters.

CATCHING A WAITER'S EYE

Q. Can you suggest a foolproof way of catching a waiter's eye? I find that when one's palate is primed to receive a particular wine or foodstuff, it can substantially decrease one's enjoyment if the waiter pretends not to see one until the moment of potential gratification has passed. As I am over-weight, and anyway rather diffident by nature, I do not like to get up from the table and be forceful about it.

H.M.M., Clanricarde Gardens, W.2

A. *Pocket tennis games for children are available from most toy shops. The ball shoots out bullet-like at the press of a button and the idea is that the child should attempt re-capture into the conical base provided – to which it is linked by elasticated string. The ball can be aimed in the direction of a passing waiter with effective results, though, of course, having thus caught the waiter's eye, you would pretend that the discharge had been accidental.*

EMBARRASSMENT WHEN WAITERS RECITE THE SPECIALS OF THE DAY

Q. Where should one look when the waiter starts to recite the specials of the day? I find it so embarrassing that it quite puts me off my meal and I can never concentrate on what he or she is saying, as I am so busy trying to nod in en-couragement to compensate for what I imagine must be their own intense embarrassment.

G.F., Bruton Street, W.1

A. *Why not interrupt the waiter before he launches into the re-citation by saying, 'I'm afraid I'm slightly deaf. Do you have them on a hand-written card by any chance?'*

PROBLEMS WITH MENUS

Menus are so pretentious these days that there is no need for anyone to worry about being unable to understand what the dishes are. Problem pages in teenage magazines were once dominated by the matter of whether or not one should admit that one did not understand the names of the dishes, but now that one can be faced with such options as 'Encirclement of the surprised pig' or 'Rocket flambe', it would actually be pre-tentious not to ask for an explanation.

DINNER AT THE GARRICK CLUB

Q. I am being taken to dinner next week by a boy I met at the

Fourth of June. We are going to the Garrick Club – but I know he is quite broke. As the prices won't be shown on my menu, how can I choose a dish that won't cripple him financially, without actually asking him which dish is cheapest?

C.C., Beaminster

A. *It is always a safe bet to plump for grapefruit- and chicken-based dishes when unsure of prices. These two items are generally guaranteed to be the cheapest on the menu. Try to avoid poussin, though, as inexperienced handling of this dish can cause embarrassment.*

SUITABLE TIMES FOR DINING

The social possibilities of dining out often count as being of at least equal, if not more, importance than the possibilities for oral stimulation. A tradition has therefore grown up that restaurants are usually at their busiest at around 9.30 each evening.

Eating the biggest meal of the day shortly before retiring strikes many socialisers as anomalous: habitually they go from around 5.00 p.m. until sometimes 10.00 p.m. feeling dizzy and weak with hunger, smoking and drinking wine and having snacks of toast or cereal until the 'proper' hour to eat comes around. Sleeping badly has become a way of life for such people, as their digestive systems struggle to break down and process the heavy loads of foodstuffs ingested shortly before climbing into bed. Many of them secretly eat at 6.00 p.m. or 7.00 p.m. when spending the evening alone.

EATING BEFORE OR AFTER THE OPERA OR CINEMA?

Q. What are the rules about times of eating when one is taking a group to the cinema or the opera as part of the evening's entertainment? Should one eat before or after?

D.M., S.W.1

A. *As the main programme in many cinemas does not now begin until 9.30 p.m., one is able, in theory, to eat in a nearby restaurant before the performance, provided, of course, that one has procured the tickets in advance. Yet many working Londoners will have difficulty in 'making' a restaurant by 7.30 or even 8.00. Some complain that dining before a performance will cause them to sleep through it.*

The best solution is to tip fellow members of the party off that they should have a snack prior to leaving home, then everyone may enjoy a light supper in the restaurant afterwards, at a meal which is taken more for the purposes of socialising than of fuelling their systems.

To Share or Not?

STOPPING OTHERS FROM HELPING THEMSELVES TO ONE'S OWN SPECIAL DISH IN A CHINESE RESTAURANT

Q. My girlfriend and I frequently patronise Yung's restaurant in Wardour Street with friends who enjoy Chinese food. There is only one problem. I find it very annoying whenever I have ordered a special dish – usually sweet and sour king prawns, to see everyone else helping themselves to it. How does one assert one's rights over certain dishes when one has agreed to share vegetables and rice, for example, and one's fellow diners rather take advantage and take from one's main dish as well?   R.R., Drayton Gardens, S.W.10

A. *Coach your girlfriend to say loudly when your special dish arrives, 'That looks really good, Rory. Can I just taste it?' You should pretend not to hear, to give her a chance to repeat it, thus ensuring everyone else gets the message that the dish is for your own private consumption.*

BILL-SPLITTING PROBLEMS

Q. Now that I am on a serious diet and am also really broke, I am beginning to resent having to split bills with people. Yesterday, for example, I was obliged to pay half of a lunch bill when I had simply had a starter course and a Perrier, while my companion enjoyed three courses and half a bottle of wine. How does one get out of this without seeming petty?
C.L., W.11

A. *When going out for a luncheon such as this it is important to leave your chequebook and card at home and carry only an amount of cash roughly commensurate to the amount you intend to consume. In this way, if you should be asked to pay for half of a bill, you can produce your money saying, 'Sorry, but I've only got £10 in cash – that's why I only had the avocado mozzarella,' or words to that effect.*

JOCULAR SUPPRESSION OF SHARED DISH BULLIES

Q. It seems to me that if you are not incredibly pushy these days you are trodden underfoot by those who are. I live with some friends in S.W.10. We regularly go to a Chinese restaurant called the Golden Duck in Hollywood Road with lots of other people. What I find irritating is that all this delicious food comes in a central pyramid for everyone to share, yet the less pushy among the company can hardly get purchase on the table-edge for their elbows, let alone help themselves. It is embarrassing to have to say anything because that only highlights the greediness of everyone else and could spoil the atmosphere.   A.B., W.8

A. *In the circumstances one should jocularly knock out of the way the chopsticks of the more bullying members of the party and thereby make a joke of your mutual urges for oral gratification.*

PROBLEMS OF COMMUNAL DISHES

Q. How can one genially upbraid someone who is helping himself too lavishly in a restaurant where the vegetables are served in a communal dish? My friend Hugh is particularly greedy and tends to be guilty of this crime. G.W., Nairobi

A. *Why not say to your friend, as he is preparing his load, 'Do finish it. I had plenty to eat last night.'? I am sure this will serve to bring him up sharp.*

METHOD FOR MAKING UNDESIRABLE FELLOW DINERS INVISIBLE

Q. I walked into a restaurant the other night to have dinner and was put at a table right next to a friend of my father's. He was dining with someone who was definitely not his wife. I studiously ignored him despite the fact that we were not more than three feet apart. Was this the right thing to do?
C.C., S.W.11

A. *Yes, up to a point. I always advise people to take careful note of whom they are about to be placed next to when approaching a table in a restaurant. When it is apparent that a difficulty is unavoidable, glasses-wearers must whip them off. Others proceed as normal. Studiously ignore, as you did, the object of your embarrassment and as early as possible announce to your dining partner in a loud voice that he will have to choose for you. You cannot read the menu, you shout, as you are as blind as a bat without your glasses. Try to look myopic throughout the meal and to be totally engrossed in your own companion. Whether or not you normally wear glasses is of no importance, as you could always have been blind but failed to wear them for reasons of vanity.*

TOO LOUD MUSIC

Q. Why do some restaurants play cacophonous modern music at unbearable levels of loudness? I am thinking in particular of some of the more inexpensive places such as hamburger and pizza outlets which are reasonably priced but where one's enjoyment is restricted by the unpleasantness of the music. L.C., S.W.3

A. *This is a deliberate policy on behalf of the restaurant to stop people from staying too long and is known as Maximum Capacity Seating. Along with uncomfortable chairs it is deliberately used to increase a restaurant's turnover of so-called covers.*

SEATING TROUBLES

TABLE-HOPPING

Q. What is the protocol about table-hopping in a restaurant? I often find when I go into a certain restaurant in Bristol (called Mackwick and Hunt) that I know a number of the other people in there. Is one supposed to stop at every table, and if so, should one sit down? J.B., Clifton

A. *No. Everyone on entering a restaurant ought to make a deliberate point of staring myopically into the middle distance. Only when you have got safely to your seat should you then take the opportunity to glance over the restaurant to make sure that there is no one you wish to talk to.*

Q. When one is dining with fashionable people oneself, and other people, whom one knows but does not wish to acknowledge for fear of lowering oneself in the estimation of the people with whom one is dining, come towards one's table, what can one do to avoid introducing them?

J.G., Park Avenue, N.Y.10012

A. *There is no need to feel embarrassed or to allow cringing movements to betray the fact that you feel any guilt. Adopt the mental attitude that everyone knows some dreadful people and it is part of life's rich tapestry. Allow the person to come up to your table and say politely, 'How are you? Antonia Pinter, Harold Pinter. Tony B . . . You can always say afterwards that you were sorry not to have asked the person to sit down but that the Pinters had taken you out to dinner.*

Gardening

THERE IS NO DOUBT that those who enjoy gardening are tormented by the tyranny inherent in the pursuit. With each area which is cleared for cultivation another job creation scheme is effected as even more weeds have to be dealt with. Yet gardening's therapeutic qualities are well proven and it is a mistake to think that, for example, retirement would be wasted in the Sysiphean struggle of keeping a garden under control. Many wonder if they should be travelling instead. Yet, as one's life expectancy is extended by gardening, so time spent in the conduct of the pursuit could be said effectively to pay for itself.

Answers to technical problems, such as growth promotion, disease and style, will be more sensibly referred to straightforward gardening experts. In this book we will look at the social problems which can arise out of ownership of a garden.

GARDENS AND NEIGHBOURS

LEYLANDII BLIGHT

Q. My next door neighbour has planted a boundary hedge of *Cyprus leylandii* which will soon grow to a monstrous height and shade my whole garden. What can I do?

J.C., Cheltenham

A. *Why not apply an effective growth inhibitor such as Cut-lass from ICI. Sprinkled on your side of the hedge, Cut-lass would soon sink to the roots of the* leylandii *and should keep this landscape-disfiguring alien in check.*

DARKENED DOORSTEP

Q. Twenty years ago a neighbour planted an orchard next to our garden. It has now overgrown and is robbing our garden of much-needed light. Unless we can persuade the owners to lop the offending branches, we might be forced to sell as we cannot stand living in perpetual gloom. What shall we do?

S.R., Minehead

A. *There is a drastic solution to which you could resort. Plant an American walnut (Juglans nigra) alongside the neighbouring orchard. This tree has the little-known capacity of poisoning other trees in the immediate vicinity, particularly fruit trees, with a substance called juglone which penetrates their roots. Apple trees near black walnuts are often known to die mysteriously. Only you would know the cause.*

CREATING A FENCE

Q. I have bought an idyllic end-of-terrace cottage in Hampshire. The locals seem friendly but, only being tenants of their cottages, have never felt the need to enclose their back gardens with fences. We are anxious not to offend them but, for privacy, and because of the local dogs, we wish to erect a fence. How should we go about this?   G.E., Hants

A. *Good fences make good neighbours. To avoid the appearance of creating a social barrier between you and them why not choose a low fence of four feet maximum so that conversations can still take place and plant a quickthorn hedge in front of it? The hedge will creep up to the desired height of six or seven feet without engendering the shock of a sudden installation of a barrier of that height.*

COMPOUND ERROR

Q. Our much-loved view of the downs has been obliterated by a newly built breeze-block cattle compound. As a farm building it needed no planning permission, which seems scandalous. This huge edifice is only feet away from our garden boundary and we can only deduce that the farmer chose this site out of churlishness because we outbid him for some adjoining land at an auction. How can we register our protest?   O.P., Worcs

A. *You could exact some revenge by planting a screen of willows in close proximity to the building. The huge root systems of these thirsty trees will soon undermine the building and render it unsafe and untenable for the future.*

For all those who are bullied by friends and partners for spending too much time in the garden, there are equal numbers who are bullied for spending insufficient time on their plot and for allowing thickening undergrowth and weedlife to take over.

One well-known syndrome which effects older people is the unhappiness their garden starts to cause for them when they begin to become less able to deal with the exacting physical strain required from them.

GARDEN GETTING ON TOP

Q. My parents, aged sixty-three and sixty-six, are talking of selling our family house in Devon because the one-acre garden is 'getting on top' of them. So many of their generation have made this mistake. How can I dissuade them?

M.W., Drewsteignton

A. *Many sixty-year-olds who give up their gardens for this reason rush swiftly down the slope into decrepitude. With more and more farmers being encouraged to join the 'Set-Aside' scheme, why not encourage your parents to stay on and let the majority of the garden turn back to meadow, providing a wildlife habitat, etc. They could then continue to cultivate, say, a quarter of the area formally.*

OTHER GARDEN-OWNERSHIP PROBLEMS

FREEDOM TO ROAM

Q. In many ways I am in complete accordance with the aims of the Freedom to Roam Society, but not when my own back yard, so to speak, comprises only half an acre. Some teenage idealists have taken to lounging there every Sunday and my family and I are finding the intrusion of privacy quite harrowing. As yet we have not acted. What should we do?

R.C., Petworth

A. *Why not approach the loungers in friendly manner and engage them in conversation which should involve the revelation of their own home addresses. As they probably live within striking distance, it may not be too inconvenient for you to return the compliment in their backyards until your point is pushed gently home.*

SWIMMING POOL BLUES

Q. I am quite fond of about three sets of neighbours who regularly ask if they can use my swimming pool, but this summer they have come too often. How can I put them off without being rude?

P.L., Walling

A. *'What a pity,' you can say, pleasantly. 'I've just thrown in the sodium hypochlorite to cleanse the pool so we can't use it.'*

A LONDON GARDEN

Q. My husband and I have always enjoyed growing a few vegetables in our large garden in Fulham but recently reports of high lead concentration in vegetables grown in London have made us think twice about eating them. However, we enjoy the satisfying process of cultivation so what can we do?

J.P., S.W.6

A. *The coarse fisherman takes pleasure from his catch yet still throws it back in the water. Why not apply the same principle to your vegetable cultivation? You can still enjoy growing and picking the vegetables and can then throw them back into the soil where they will no doubt rot down to produce good humus for next year's crop.*

Cultural confusion over the condition of 'Workman's Buttock'.

DRESS

NOW THAT FASHION IS DEAD and 'correct' costume is worn mainly by the middle classes, the subject of what one is going to wear to key functions no longer racks the nerves in the way it once did.

Haute bohemians and the titled make fashion statements of their own when they attend formal functions. This was witnessed recently by the thousands of well-wishers who thronged Gloucester Cathedral for the wedding of Isabella Delves Broughton and Detmar Blow. They observed the appearance of some of our pre-eminent noblemen in such unceremonial items as loud check suits, lime green shirts, mini-skirts and velvet top hats.

In fact, it is fair to say that the *sine qua non* of a modern young aristocrat is to have at least one little flourish, one snook-cock against convention. Like Lord Neidpath he might wear frock coats and cravats on every occasion; like the Honourable David Herbert, a djellaba; like Lord Londonderry he might sport a one-pound coin dispenser on his belt. It might even be said that the *wrong* clothes are the mark of a gentleman, yet it is still important to make oneself as physically attractive as possible for public events.

Being physically attractive pays obvious dividends. Not only does it ensure a free-flowing flood of further invitations, which will enable one to boost one's self-esteem and consume excellent foodstuffs and drinks, it will also serve as a safeguard against falling prey to cruel romantic partners whose only aim is to reduce the self-esteem of others in order to compensate for their own feelings of inadequacy.

For those who actually have no attractive clothing at all, let alone the 'correct' clothing, the following advice may be useful.

NON-POSSESSION OF ATTRACTIVE CLOTHING

Q. Although my family are only minor diplomats, their long sojourns abroad have occasioned me to be educated at St Mary's Calne. This sometimes gives people the wrong impression about my own status. I met a young man recently who belongs to one of our leading ducal families. He has asked me to spend Easter with his family in Northumberland. I have literally nothing to wear and no money with which to buy something.   A.C., W.8

A. *Travel by train to Northumberland bearing only hand luggage and your most attractive outfit. Stepping lightly down from the train, greet your welcomers warmly, then say vaguely that your luggage was stolen on the way. Not only will you have a fool-proof excuse for being badly dressed but you will be loaned clothing, probably of an extremely high quality, which will enhance your appearance – or even excuse it.*

BORROWING CLOTHING FROM OTHERS

It must not be forgotten that clothing can often be borrowed from other people. Borrowing clothes as a phenomenon grew up in the hippy period and is still a widespread cultural practice. One can equally go to outlets such as The Gallery of Antique Textiles in Lisson Grove and purchase items of extreme beauty at one-third of the price of a new couture outfit.

LENDING DIFFICULTIES

Q. As I spend most of my money on clothes, I do tend to have more beautiful dresses, many of them antique, than most of my girlfriends. It is not that I mind lending them out for 'special' occasions, which seem to happen every two weeks, but that my friends often aren't very careful with them. How can I say no or at least ensure that they are returned in good condition?   C.L., W.11

A. *Why not say that your dresses are on loan to the V & A's modern costume department? 'I may have one or two that I haven't sent over yet,' you can relent. 'But they must come back almost as though they haven't been worn.'*

TIPPING FRIENDS OFF THAT THEIR CLOTHING IS UNATTRACTIVE

No one likes to be the bearer of bad news. It is distressing to see the looks on the wounded one's face. But worse than that, one becomes irrevocably linked in that person's mind with displeasure and so it can ultimately be a self-damaging act to help a friend by tipping them off frankly about their visual offensiveness. More indirect means need to be undertaken.

PHOTOGRAPHIC EVIDENCE

Q. My friend Sarah has the most enormous bottom. When she wears trousers she looks great from the front but appalling from behind. I don't think she realises this. How should I tell her without making her hate me? She is wearing trousers more and more because we have started to go to quite a few cricket matches to watch my brother. K.W., Maidenhead

A. *Why not simply take some photographs at the next cricket match, composing your shot carefully to show your friend's bottom in all it's enormity as only the secondary subject of the photographs? You can then leave the photographs lying around for her to look at.*

SANDALLED FOOTWEAR

Q. My father, aged sixty-four, is a poet and former beatnik. He is wonderful in every way except one – he wears sandals whenever possible and is planning to give me away at my forthcoming wedding, in sandals. How can I prevent him from wearing them without hurting his feelings?

J.F., W.12

A. *Why not ask him to wear shoes on grounds of personal safety? Explain that one close friend, who will be present at the wedding reception, will be accompanied by his dog, which, though generally obedient, reacts with ferocity to the sound of sandalled feet; this is because of a traumatic incident in its puppyhood.*

Other sartorial offences which should be avoided at all costs include having a 'bottom' on one's chest – a mistake often made by the large-busted in decollete – and the highlighting of a flat bottom by the wearing of trousers or clinging skirting. Flat-bottomed girls can make use of buttock-perters, which are curvature-enhancing pads, available at Rigby & Peller, corsetieres to HM The Queen, Hans Place, S.W.1. They can be sewn into clothing just above the 'start' of the bottom to give a pleasing African appearance to one's rear view.

Accessories

Q. I have always thought it would be frightfully amusing to have a cuckoo watch. Despite numerous enquiries amongst watchsmiths, however, I have come to a complete impasse. It appears that most watches are mass-made and the manufacturers I have spoken to seem generally unprepared to try out a run of cuckoo watches. Can you recommend someone who would be willing to custom-make such an item for me?

N.D., Durham

A. *You might try Henry Bowler-Reed of Time Restored in Pewsey, Wiltshire. He is an antiquarian horologist with a sideline in motorised oddments and may be interested in helping fulfil your ambition.*

Showing Off Lovely Underwear

Q. My grandmother has given me some incredibly beautiful silk underwear which was part of her wedding trousseau in the 1920s. How can I show it off at a forthcoming houseparty in Scotland without it being obvious that I am showing it off? Would it be acceptable to wander the corridors in underwear at bathtime?

C.C., S.W.11

A. *Obstacles to the successful 'pulling off' of a corridor display include mammoth co-ordination difficulties and the distinct possibility that your bathroom will be en suite. A more effective means of display would in any case be to persuade fellow guests to take part in the popular after-dinner game Swopstop. Players stand next to a member of the opposite sex. Lights are turned out for a decreasing number of minutes during which participants struggle to exchange all clothing except underwear with successive partners and present themselves, with buttons and zips done up, when the lights come on. The game affords marvellous opportunities for the display of underwear.*

Peter Jones

Q. I find it absolutely maddening to have to queue with a numbered ticket in the shoe department at Peter Jones every time I want to have my son fitted with new shoes. Why can't they simply take on more staff?

J.F., Balham, near London

A. *Peter Jones' management claims that there is always a rush just before certain schools go back, but, because they provide a service by qualified fitters who go on a course and get a qualification, they cannot simply bring in staff from another department. Chelsea dwellers, however, have long complained that Peter Jones is 'never knowingly over-staffed'.*

CULTURAL MISUNDERSTANDINGS

Q. I am a stranger to this country. I come from Japan and my husband has come here to work in a bank. Our new house is being decorated and I am very shocked because all the workmen show their bottoms to me. Is this mooning? Should I tell my husband? What should I do?   K.N., S.W.1

A. *It is highly unlikely that the workman in your house are 'mooning'. Mooning, where the entire buttock area is displayed to a shocked onlooker, is practised by lower-level Britons as a form of insult. All British workmen, on the other hand, suffer from a condition known as 'Workman's Buttock' where the waist – expanded disproportionately to accommodate an unnecessarily large amount of beer – becomes too large for the waistband of the trousers. The trousers therefore slip downwards with the consequent display of at least half the so-called 'crack' of any workman's buttock.*

I have been provoked beyond endurance by my girlfriend's teddy bears.

Emergencies

NOT ALL THE LIKELY EMERGENCIES which may face a socialiser can possibly be dealt with in these pages. We can, however, look at some of the leading causes of unexpected anxiety which have afflicated certain correspondents and the possible solutions which have been suggested.

Getting Out of Jury Service

Q. How can I get out of doing jury service? It really is coming at a most inconvenient time and I understand that one is obliged by law to attend. A.S., W.1

A. *One method you could attempt would be to reply to your 'call-up' papers in an excessive vein. Announce that you will be only too glad to assist in ridding the country of vermin and that you have long stood for flogging and capital punishment and the repatriation of foreign nationals. One unwilling juror who did this was pleased to receive a cancellation notice in the next post informing him that his services would no longer be required.*

Stopping Oneself From Laughing in Church

Q. My problem is that when a situation requires that one simply mustn't laugh on any account, such as in church, then the tears begin to course down my cheeks and I start to shake with uncontrollable hysteria. In the past I have twice had to leave mid-sermon because of this problem. I am now going out with someone whose family are fairly big landowners in Suffolk and consequently are regular worshippers at their village church. How can I control myself when I too am required to attend a service? I.L.S., S.W.10

A. *Why not put on a pair of lace-up shoes two sizes too small for you just before entering the church. The agonising pain should begin in earnest as you take your pew and should act as an extremely effective suppressant of laughter. Provided they are removed shortly after the service the damage should not be long-lasting.*

DIFFICULT DOGS

Q. My problem concerns a gun dog named Nimble, owned by my grandfather, which is causing embarrassment to the whole family. Nimble is an ageing and massively overweight golden retriever who can no longer sniff scents nor scamper enthusiastically to retrieve pheasants. He limps, smells, occasionally bites a beater and at the end of the day has to be carried home. How can we suggest that the dog be retired without hurting my grandfather's feelings? The invitations are beginning to dry up and family friction is mounting.

P.M., Easton Neston

A. *Many delinquent dogs, both senile and juvenile, cause nuisances while their owners remain blind to their defects. Though personally sympathetic to your grandfather and his dog, I suppose action is necessary and suggest you take the following step. Purchase an uncostly supply of so-called 'stink bombs' from a joke shop. In the field you should break them open at regular intervals and pretend that the gases are being emitted from the dog's rectal region. Show concern and, once home, pretend to have contracted an emergency veterinary service as your grandfather's own vet is unobtainable. At this point a paid student actor should enter the room posing as a vet and break the sad news to your grandfather that the dog is really too old for active service and should be allowed to live out his days on the comfort of a hearthrug.*

STOPPING ONE'S SON FROM DROPPING OUT OF SCHOOL BEFORE TAKING HIS A-LEVELS.

Q. My eighteen-year-old son has been doing well at his public school, but now he wants to leave before sitting his A-levels in June. It is all because he is taking a 'moral stand' over the issue of whether or not he should have a ridiculous little tuft of hair at the back of his neck cut. It has become a battle of wills between James and his headmaster and neither is prepared to stand down. I am at my wits' end. I have explained to James that he will effectively ruin his life by not taking his

A-levels, but he is immoveable. What can I do?

T.B., Malaga

A. *The peak moments of hormonal activity in the developing youth do, unfortunately, coincide with key examinations. Many intelligent schoolboys 'make stands' just before their A-levels and inexperience is an effective antidote to reason.*

The only solution is a simple bribe. Offer him the sum of £3000 to have the tuft cut and finish his A-levels. This is roughly half what you would spend next year on tutorial fees and is a staggeringly impressive sum to a schoolboy. This solution was used with success on one Etonian last year and the mothers of his errant contemporaries bitterly regretted that they had not adopted the same measure.

GETTING AWAY FROM SKINHEADS

May I offer you some advice which your readers may find useful in the event of their being surrounded by a gang of skinheads at dead of night, a position in which I found myself on a recent visit to Chelsea? I was always under the impression that the backstreets of Chelsea were completely safe after about twelve o'clock, as one would normally expect that gangs of ruffians would have had to leave the area by then in order to catch the last tube. I had had dinner in Tedworth Square and was walking towards Smith Street on my way to my own London flat in Wellington Square when, rounding the corner, I saw to my abject horror a gang of about forty skinheads coming towards me.

Knowing that flight was impossible, I made a split-second decision. Pulling my face into a palsy-style grimace, I dragged one of my legs, polio-boot style, behind me. The skinheads courteously cleared a path and I limped safely through.

K.K., Wellington Square

CULLING FRIENDS

Q. Is there such a thing as culling friends? Now that I am thirty-six and have been amassing friends since schooldays, I feel menaced by the conflicting demands of so many different people. I feel I am going to have simply to say to people, 'Look I just can't see you more than twice a year, if that.' But how should I go about it?

M.K., Marlborough, Wilts

A. *This seems a rather hysterical measure. Why not have a cooling-off period of a month or two, where you pretend to be ill or abroad. When you re-enter social life you could restrict your activities to big parties thrown once a month at which you could 'work off' many friends in one fell swoop.*

DESTRUCTION OF A FAVOURED TEDDY BEAR

Q. I am a student at UEA. I have a girlfriend reading environmental studies who is currently doing field work in Egypt. I am dreading her return as, during her absence, I destroyed her main teddy bear in a fit of temper. I was fed up with sharing the bed with it and about thirty other toys. I now regret it, mainly because I know she will not forgive me. I do not want to split up with her, yet how can I possibly explain the mysterious disappearance of a mangy old teddy bear, without telling her the truth?   A.C., Norwich

A. *Anyone who watches 'University Challenge' on television will see that students seem to have a rather childish confidence in toys as lucky mascots. There is no reason why you yourself should not have taken the bear along as a mascot to some similar event where it was kidnapped by another student from a rival university. 'All I know is that she rang the Student's Union to apologise,' you can say. 'She said she had fallen in love with it and would give it a happy home, but she refused to give her name.'*

ARRIVAL OF A GROUP OF FOREIGNERS ON ONE'S DOORSTEP

Q. My husband is a housemaster at a well-known public school and has consistently, throughout his tenure, been extremely popular with the boys. As he is a personal tutor we have obviously become rather close to certain boys who have come to tea in our own home at least once a week when we have discussed all manner of topics. That is all very well, but some of these boys are of European or South American origin and we have increasingly experienced the problem of finding our doorbell rung at odd hours of the day and opening it to find groups of up to six young people, aged eighteen to twenty, standing in anticipation on our doorstep, pronouncing our names and saying that they have been told by our former charges, now back in their lands of origin, they should call and say hello to us. They clearly expect to be invited in and entertained over up to three or four days.

What can we do? We clearly cannot bang the door in their faces as one would with a double-glazing salesman, as they are all very nice, idealistic youths. But we simply cannot process the numbers who are arriving on a weekly basis.

(Name and address withheld)

A. *First, you should always be prepared for the eventuality of finding such people on your doorstep when you open it. If your worst fears are justified and a group of foreigners are waiting there in anticipation, you should adopt the following measure. Beam ecstatically at all those who are on the doorstep and say, enthusiastically, 'I am so pleased and honoured that you have called.' Holding the front door ajar behind you, you should then shake the hand of each foreigner in turn while expressing an individual sentiment such as, 'I hope very much that you will enjoy your visit', 'I am extremely happy to meet a cousin of Fredericos', or 'How lovely to see you in our country'. When you have finished shaking hands with them you may stand back in a friendly but dispatching stance and say, 'Thank you so much for calling. I hope you have a very happy holiday in our country.' Nod and smile vehemently while issuing this sentiment. With any luck the students will be confused into thinking that this brief form of welcome is the custom in England.*

PEOPLE RINGING FROM CALLBOXES SAYING THEY ARE IN THE AREA

Q. My husband and I have been travelling a lot over the past ten years and as a result we have amassed an enormous number of friends from all parts of the globe. What we find difficult is the fact that at least three times a month we receive a call from a phone box, and someone we have met while travelling abroad has turned up in England and is keen to see us. So many of these people are in England for only a couple of days and it seems churlish not to cancel whatever else we might be doing in order to fit them in. But for obvious reasons, we cannot simply fit them into our schedule at the drop of a hat. Have you any solution?

N.S., Debden, Suffolk

A. *The late David McEwen had a successful solution for dealing with such a problem. On receipt of the call, either from a foreigner arriving at Heathrow or Gatwick, or even from someone ringing from a call box 'in the area' he would say with enthusiasm, 'How brilliant. Come now!'*

It is very rare that any of these people would be able to come immediately, even though they are ringing from a call box. And if they are unable to come then the guilt will be shifted onto their plates.

GETTING INTO ACTING SCHOOL

Q. I am shortly to make my third attempt to get into drama school. Can you suggest any way in which I can stand out from the rest of the students during the auditioning process?

C.P., Longleat

A. *Yes. Why not make the investment of hiring the Sir John Gielgud lookalike from the Lookalikes Model Agency in Paternoster Row. Instruct him to sit at the back of the theatre during your own audition and rise to his feet in rapturous applause as your performance comes to a close. He should then slip swiftly out of the building.*

NEWSPAPER PHOBIA

Q. I am one of the richest men in the country, yet one small thing is completely ruining my life. I am becoming increasingly depressed by the volume of newsprint that comes into my house every day. I have this terrible feeling of anxiety that I may miss something by my favourite journalists if I don't sift through it all. The *Sunday Times* on its own is now so big as to be actually intrusive.

P.G., W.1

A. *Just as the government has satisfied farmers with its Set-Aside scheme, whereby fields are left unfarmed to prevent crop mountains, why not start your own Set-Aside scheme for journalists? Write to your favourites asking if they would be willing to join the scheme and stop writing in exchange for being paid vast subsidies to fund their lifestyles.*

TODDLER RELIEF

Q. Can you recommend a method for keeping toddlers occupied when one has had to bring them along to key meetings, such as with one's bank manager or dressmaker?

M.B., S.W.11

A. *Many people have forgotten about the possibilities for distraction held by an old-fashioned magnet. Magnets can be purchased in hardware stores and mothers can gain relief from toddlers by the job creation scheme of spilling a box of pins about a room. The mother then offers the toddler the magnet on the end of a piece of string and requests that it uses this device to recover the pins at its earliest convenience.*

OPERA

Q. I am shortly to attend a performance of a new Michael Tippett opera. Can you recommend a personal stereo which will not irritate fellow members of the audience with its buzzing? H.F., S.W.7

A. *It is not the apparatus itself which so provokes others in public places but the ill-fitting headphones which allow the buzzing to be emitted. The new Fontopia range of headphones by Sony fit unobtrusively inside the ears and are successfully used by the growing numbers of people who wish to attend the opera for social reasons but do not wish to undergo the discomfort of actually listening to the performance.*

MEMORIAL SERVICE

Q. I regularly attend memorial services in the hope of seeing my name in print in the court pages of *The Times* or *Daily Telegraph*. Although I always make a point of giving my name quite clearly to the person on the door, I find I am constantly disappointed when it fails to appear on the following day. How can I ensure that my time is not wasted again? F.B., S.W.1

A. *As many people become serial killers simply in order to see their name in print, it seems rather unfair that a harmless urge to appear in a list of up to two hundred names should not be gratified. One method of ensuring that your name will appear is to inform the name-taker on your arrival that you are representing a body of some significance. Why not say that you are representing Christ Church College, for example? It would be virtually impossible to prove the contrary and no court page official would dream of querying such an assertion.*